Three Centuries of Jewish Life in America

Three Centuries of Jewish Life in America

Carl Lowe

MALLARD
PRESS

A FRIEDMAN GROUP BOOK

Published by MALLARD PRESS
An Imprint of BDD Promotional Book Company, Inc.
666 Fifth Avenue
New York, New York 10103

Mallard Press and its accompanying design and logo are
trademarks of BDD Promotional Book Company, Inc.

ISBN 0-7924-5778-1

THREE CENTURIES OF JEWISH LIFE IN AMERICA
was prepared and produced by
Michael Friedman Publishing Group, Inc.
15 West 26th Street
New York, New York 10010

Editors: Stephen Williams & Kelly Matthews
Art Direction: Devorah Levinrad
Designer: Maria Mann
Photography Editor: Ede Rothaus
Photography Research: Grace How

Typeset by Classic Type, Inc.
Color separations by United South Sea Graphic Art Co.
Printed and bound in Hong Kong by Leefung-Asco Printers Ltd.

Dedication

This book is dedicated to my grandparents and my children
—the past and the future of North American Jewry.

Acknowledgments

Thanks to Kelly Matthews and Stephen Williams for guiding
this book from its beginnings to its final incarnation.

Table of

Contents

Although historians still debate Columbus' religious background (he may have been Jewish), it is certain that sailors of Jewish descent accompanied him on his voyage.

Introduction

Ever since Columbus sailed to the New World, Jewish people have emigrated to the Americas, where they've played an important role in the settlement of North America and the evolution of its two great democracies —Canada and the United States.

It is ironic that the very year of Columbus' voyage—1492—was also the year that the Jews were banished from Spain. At virtually the very moment Jews were exiled from one of their primary centers of culture, learning, and prosperity, Columbus was paving the way to what would become an avenue of escape to a new home safer and more protected than any the Jewish people had known for a millennia: North America. It is fitting that Jews found such a comfortable home in the New World, for some historians say that the way was opened by means of property stolen from them; that the Spanish royalty financed Columbus' explorations with money from the sale of confiscated Jewish land and belongings.

Some claim that Columbus himself was Jewish or was a descendant of the Marranos, Spanish Jews who had converted to Christianity under the threat of death or banishment. While there is no concrete evidence to support this assertion and in fact many knowledgeable historians say it is false, it is certain that at least one Jew accompanied Columbus on his first voyage to the New World.

The first member of Columbus' crew to set foot on the soil of the New World is believed to have been his interpreter—Luis de Torres, a man who was descended from Spanish Jews. Torres spoke at least four languages, none of which was of the slightest help in communicating with the natives of the Western Hemisphere. But Torres, through signs and ingenuity, was able to make himself understood by the Amerindians on the islands where Columbus landed. Eventually, Torres became the first European tobacco plantation owner in the New World. He took one look—and sniff—at what the natives were smoking (tobacco was unknown in Europe) and saw his entrepreneurial opportunity. Soon he established his own tobacco-growing industry in what was later called Cuba. He was the first to export this habit-forming substance from the New World to the Old. As the Europeans became hooked on the aromatic weed, Torres and other tobacco growers prospered.

The Spanish banishment of Jews in 1492 was actually the inhuman conclusion to what had been a long list of Spanish anti-Jewish actions. In an effort to create a purely Christian country and grow richer from the seizure of Jewish property, Spain drove out Jewish craftsmen and scientists who could have been useful as the country climbed to the top of world power. For instance, Columbus was aided by Jewish astronomers and mapmakers as well as Jewish citizens who made nautical navigational instruments. Once Spain turned the full fury of the Inquisition on the Jews, this country forfeited a major part of its intelligentsia. Thus, much of the Old World's loss became the New World's gain.

It would be silly, of course, to insist that the rise and fall of European nations can be explained entirely by Jewish migration, and it is also true that Christian persecution of Jews also took place in the Western Hemisphere. But in general terms, the New World, and specifically North America, has proved to be an inviting haven for Jews. So much so, that today it would be hard to imagine the social landscape in such countries as the United States and Canada without their Jewish communities.

10

CHAPTER ONE

The Jews in New Amsterdam and the Early Colonies

From almost the very beginning, New York City—or New Amsterdam as it was called when ruled by the Dutch—has been a deal maker's dream as well as a home for North American Jews. The colony was begun in 1624 by the Dutch West India Company. The land on Manhattan Island was bought by Peter Minuit from Amerindians for trinkets that historians estimate were worth twenty-four dollars.

Despite what seems to have been a bargain price, questions have been raised about how sharp a real estate transaction Minuit really made. For one thing, Minuit, director general of the tract of land the Dutch called New Netherland, had to pay twice for the isle of Manhattan. The first Amerindians he bought it from were not the true owners, they were actually transients who eagerly took Minuit's offer for what wasn't theirs to convey. After these con men absconded with the jewelry, Minuit had to deliver another set of accessories to the Amerindians who held the true title.

Europeans were slow to populate New Amsterdam. By the time the first group of Jewish people arrived in the 1650s, the settlement's inhabitants numbered only about eight hundred. But like Minuit's purchase, the circumstances of the first substantial arrival of Jewish settlers in New Amsterdam also involved convoluted wheeling and dealing.

The first New Amsterdam Jews were actually refugees from South America who had intended to return to Europe. It took a series of misadventures to strand them at the mouth of the Hudson River. In the spring of 1654, the Portuguese had invaded and seized control of the town of Recife in Brazil, taking it away from the Dutch. Under the Dutch, who had originally pilfered Recife from the Portuguese in 1630, the Jews of the region had enjoyed prosperity and relative freedom. But the reconquering Portuguese, peeved because the Jews had sided with the Dutch against them, ordered the Jews out of the country.

The Recife Jewish community decided to sail back to Holland in a convoy of sixteen boats, but only fifteen made it to Europe. According to some historians, one of the ships in the group blew off course and wandered into waters frequented by pirate vessels. The pirates took everything off the ship worth stealing, sank the ship, imprisoned the twenty-three Jewish passengers, and planned to sell them as slaves.

The pirate ship in turn was captured by a French vessel, the *St. Charles*. The French captain took the Jewish passengers to the closest port on his map: New Amsterdam. Once there, he held two of the Jews hostage until the other twenty-one came up with the money to pay him for the rescue and transportation. History is not clear on how the ransom money was raised, but somehow it was, and New Amsterdam had twenty-three new residents. This meant the town had a Jewish population of twenty-five, since two others, Jacob Barsimson and Solomon Paeterson, had recently arrived. In the opinion of Peter Stuyvesant, the colony's governor, that added up to twenty-five too many. He ordered them to leave. They refused. To Stuyvesant, a crusty old member of the Dutch Reformed Church, Jews were undesirables. They may not have been at the top of his list of enemies, but they were in the top five, along with Catholics, Lutherans, Quakers, and Baptists.

Stuyvesant wrote to the Dutch West India Company asking permission to forcefully banish "this deceitful race—blasphemers of Christ." In his letter, Stuyvesant argued that if the Jews were allowed to stay, pretty soon he would have to let in Baptists and Lutherans.

While Stuyvesant was writing his letter, the Jews in question received some aid from Jews across the sea in Amsterdam, and their admonitions on behalf of the New World Jews proved to be more persuasive than Stuyvesant's letters. Several important stockholders of the Dutch West India Company were Jewish, and they wanted to trade with the Jews in New Amsterdam—a small fact Stuyvesant seems to have overlooked or thought he could ignore—and they threatened to take Jewish business elsewhere. After all, Stuyvesant wasn't threatening green-horns. These refugees had been experienced merchants in Brazil. They knew the ins and outs of trading and doing business in the New World. If the Dutch didn't want them, there were other places they could go.

In the battle of transatlantic letters, Stuyvesant lost. To the directors of the company, money, of course, spoke louder than Stuyvesant's prejudices. The directors were not about to jeopardize the Jewish dollars invested in their company simply because Peter Stuyvesant did not want Jews in his midst. And, in any case, it would have been out of character for the Dutch to refuse to allow the Jews to stay. Overall, their record for tolerance of other peoples and religions has been fairly wide-ranging and easygoing.

In those times, however, admission to the colony didn't guarantee the right to full citizenship. The Jewish settlers were allowed to establish their own cemetery in 1656 but were denied permission to build a house of worship. (The Chatham Square Cemetery still exists and is one of the oldest Jewish cemeteries in the United States.) Generally, New Amsterdam's Jews were allowed the same rights as Catholics and Lutherans—which weren't many. Private worship at home was allowed; public gatherings for worship were not.

At this time, Jews technically were not allowed to be retailers or craftsmen. Still, some historians believe that because of the shortage of skilled workers, these restrictive regulations were often ignored.

Long before Jewish settlers in New Amsterdam were permitted to build a synagogue (Shearith Israel wasn't built until 1730), permission was granted to build a cemetery. The Chatham Square cemetery, one of the oldest Jewish cemeteries in the United States, was founded in 1656.

The civic-minded Jews were soon pushing for more rights. Stuyvesant and the town council resisted. A step toward full citizenship would mean the right to stand guard with the other town "burghers" at the north wall of New Amsterdam along Wall Street. Jacob Barsimson and Asser Levy (the latter was one of the twenty-three Jews who had arrived on the *St. Charles*) applied for permission to carry out this responsibility. The town council refused, telling the Jews to "depart whenever and whither it please them."

Once again, letters crossed the Atlantic, and once again, the Jews were allowed to have what they wanted. The Dutch West India Company ruled that they could stand watch at the north end of town. Then, in 1656, the company gave Stuyvesant a bureaucratic slap on the wrist for giving the Jewish colonists such a hard time. The directors ruled that Jews could actually own their own pieces of the New World and become property owners. They were also allowed to engage in crafts trades and barter furs and goods in most sections of New Netherland, including Albany (which at the time was called Fort Orange). The permission to trade was important, since the major commercial activity was fur trading. The most lucrative business of all was the business in beaver pelts, which were in great demand in Europe.

Once the commercial chains began to be unlocked, talented Jewish businessmen like Asser Levy began to acquire wealth and status. In time, Levy soon became a full-fledged burgher—a citizen with all rights. Thus, in 1657, Levy had the honor of being the first such full-privileged Jewish citizen in colonial North America. When he bought property on William Street, Levy was also probably the first Jewish landowner in what eventually became the United States. He also owned land in Fort Orange, and as part of his high status, he became one of New Amsterdam's six licensed butchers in 1660. As an official butcher, he was exempt from having to cut up nonkosher animals.

The British Takeover

In 1664, the British, with their superior naval and military forces, took New Amsterdam away from the Dutch and renamed it New York. At the same time, they named the mainland on the other side of the Hudson River New Jersey. Initially, after England took over, it was unclear whether the new rulers would prove to be more or less tolerant than the Dutch. Once again, the Jews were in the position of depending on the kindness of strangers.

It transpired that the Jews had little to worry about. Apparently, business considerations and the fact that the Jews were so well-established in New Amsterdam convinced the British to leave the Jewish population more or less alone. The New World was large and there weren't enough skilled people to populate it and the

Moses Levy (left) was a prominent Jewish merchant who arrived in New York in the 1690s. His fleet of ships (opposite) earned him large sums in the import and export trade.

American Jewish Archives

talent of the Jewish settlers was desired. The result was that the Jews were actually allowed to engage in public worship, a step that led to the erection of New York's first synagogue.

Under British rule, Asser Levy's entrepreneurial enterprises continued to prosper. He lent the Lutherans the money to build their first church in 1671. He made money as the municipal guardian of goods subject to litigation. In 1678, he built a public slaughterhouse on Wall Street. (Later, investors in the stock market would be slaughtered financially on just about the same spot.)

As for Peter Stuyvesant, after the British took away his power, the unyielding tormentor of the Jews and other minorities in New Amsterdam lived out his final years on his farm on the Lower East Side of Manhattan in a section called the Bouwerie—later to be anglicized as the Bowery. In the first half of this century, millions of Jews from Eastern Europe found their first American homes in the tenements of the Lower East Side that stand on land that used to be his fields. When he died in 1672, Stuyvesant was buried in the chapel that later became St. Mark's Church in the Bowery.

Under the British, some of the religious restrictions the Dutch had imposed were gradually relaxed. By 1682, Jews were no longer limited to worshiping in private homes. They could rent a house for public prayer. Shearith Israel—the Remnant of Israel—located on Mill Street, was dedicated as the first Jewish synagogue on Passover in 1730. Now located uptown on Central Park West in the Spanish and Portuguese Synagogue, a Shearith Israel congregation still gathers and is considered the oldest congregation in the United States.

Strangely enough, after England seized control of New Amsterdam, many of the Jews living in what had become New York still thought of themselves as Dutch. These Jews stubbornly continued to speak Dutch, decorated their houses with Dutch-style furniture, and generally considered anything British as déclassé.

Other Jews welcomed the British with open arms. Some even took up arms for them during King William's War, a conflict fought from 1689 to 1697. Many Jews anglicized their names, changing their Spanish surnames into the English equivalents. For instance, the common Jewish name Pardo was frequently translated as Brown.

With British rule, more Ashkenazi Jews from England also arrived. (Sephardi Jews are generally from Spain and Portugal, while Ashkenazi Jews are from other parts of Europe.) One prominent immigrant was Moses Levy (no relation to Asser Levy), who came over in the 1690s. Unlike some of the other penniless immigrants who worked their way up to prominence in the colonies, Levy was already well-to-do when he first stepped onto the streets of New York. He used his money to establish himself quickly as a landowner, slave trader, and ship owner. Much of his money came from the fur trade. He and his children formed a formidable financial dynasty.

This Levy family didn't confine their commercial activities to the New York area. As the Europeans spread across the continent, so did the Levys and their

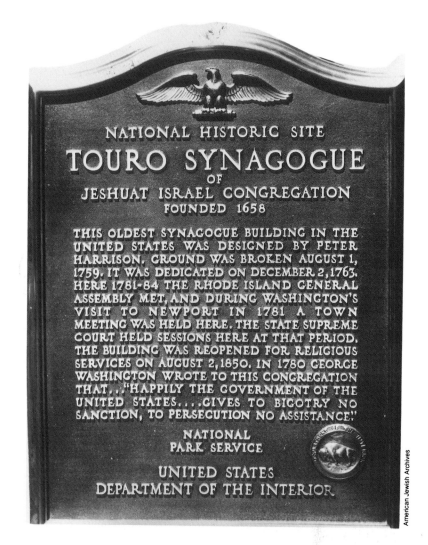

The Spanish and Portuguese synagogue (left), home to the Shearith Israel congregation, was redecorated in 1948 by "Jack" Fidanaue. This plaque (above) commemorates the Touro Synagogue's status as the oldest synagogue building in the United States. The Newport, Rhode Island, edifice was dedicated in 1763.

American Jewish Archives

The Touro synagogue was designed by Peter Harrison, the same architect who built the King's Chapel in Boston. Today, visitors can still visit this landmark in Newport, Rhode Island.

Jewish neighbors from New York and the other seaboard towns. One of Moses Levy's sons, Haym Levy, became the richest fur trader in the thirteen British colonies, bartering pelts that had been shipped from as far away as the wilds of Ohio and Kentucky.

John Jacob Astor, founder of the great Astor fortune, got his first job from Haym Levy. The young Astor made a dollar a day cleaning furs. Similarly, Levy hired Nicholas Low as a clerk, who in turn amassed his own wealth and gave shape to another influential family. One of his descendants was Seth Low, a president of Columbia University on Manhattan's Upper West Side from 1890 to 1901.

Rhode Island Welcomes Jewish Settlement

While the Jews of colonial New York formed the predominant early Jewish community, there was Jewish settlement and sociological impact up and down the Atlantic coast. In 1733, for example, James Oglethorpe and friends started a colony to aid English paupers in what is now Georgia. Although not all the partners agreed with the policy, Jews were admitted. Later on, the founders were glad they did. One of these Jewish arrivals, a doctor named Samuel Nuñez, was credited with virtually singlehandedly fighting off an epidemic.

Second to New York, the most significant initial colonial Jewish community was formed in Rhode Island. It is not surprising that this colony was a comfortable home for Jews—according to Roger Williams, the founding father of Rhode Island, the colony was designed to be a bastion of religious freedom.

In 1635, the Massachusetts Bay Colony had ousted Williams specifically because of his radical views on religious tolerance. Soon after he and his followers founded Rhode Island (settling mostly in Newport), fifteen Jewish families arrived from the Netherlands and joined these settlers. In the late 1670s, these Jews founded their own cemetery. Along with the Chatham cemetery in New York, this is one of the oldest Jewish cemeteries in the United States.

Unfortunately, when Roger Williams died in 1683, some of the religious tolerance of the community died with him. In 1685, some Christian merchants sued to have the Jews thrown out and their property confiscated. The Jews won in court, but the legal battle taught them not to take their freedom and prosperity for granted.

By the second half of the eighteenth century, Newport's Jewish residents had firmly established themselves in a booming import and export trade (rum and molasses from the West Indies were in large demand). On top of that, the town was also prospering from a bustling whaling business. The Newport reputation for wealth grew so large that other Jewish communities not so well off as the Rhode Islanders frequently came into town looking for money they could borrow.

By 1759, the Newport Jewish community was ready for its first synagogue, and it was completed in 1763. One of the colonies' best-known architects, Peter

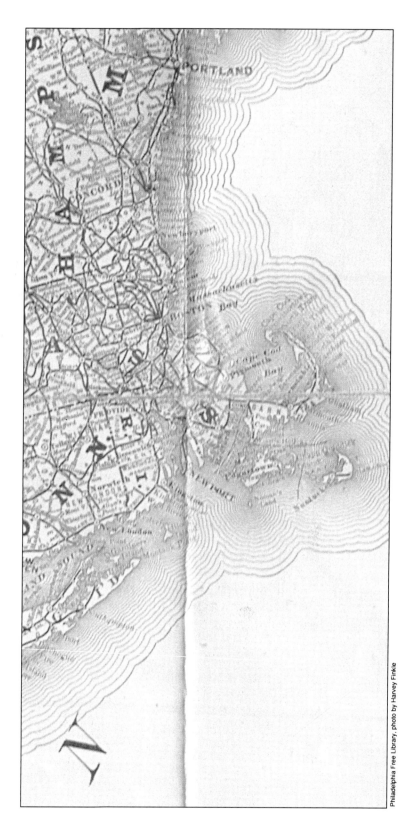

Philadelphia Free Library, photo by Harvey Finkle

American Jewish Archives

At the height of his prosperity in the pre-Revolutionary War era, Aaron Lopez of Newport, Rhode Island, owned a fleet of three dozen ships. During the war between the colonies and Great Britain, however, his ships were confiscated by the British because he supported the patriots.

Harrison (who designed the King's Chapel in Boston), designed the synagogue for the congregation Jeshuat Israel—the Salvation of Israel. The temple, now known as the Touro Synagogue (the Touro family made the bequest that has maintained the building during the last one hundred years), is a national U.S. historic shrine.

One of Newport's most intriguing Jewish residents was Aaron Lopez, whose life resembled the American Horatio Alger myth, although the myth wouldn't be established until well after Lopez's death. Lopez was born in 1724 in Portugal. His parents were Marranos who secretly worshiped as Jews, although they pretended to be Christians to avoid the Inquisition.

At this time, a notorious practice in Spain and Portugal was the auto-da-fé: the burning at the stake of heretics and nonbelievers. Pretending to be Christian while actually doubting the Church was considered to be the worst crime. Being a former Jew or the descendant of Jews was a dangerous situation. Many converted Jews were denounced by those who envied the Marranos' social position or wealth.

After witnessing too many of these barbaric executions, Lopez decided he wanted to profess openly his Jewish beliefs in a safer locale. Since his half brother Moses already lived in Newport, his destination was easy to choose. In 1752 he sailed across the Atlantic from Lisbon.

Although he did not enjoy early commercial success in Newport, he was renowned as an active and devout member of the Jewish community. When it came time for someone to lay the cornerstone for the temple, Lopez was chosen.

It wasn't until after his first wife died in 1762 and he married the daughter of one of the richest merchants in Newport that Lopez's fortune grew to astounding proportions. He soon parlayed these resources into a fleet of almost three dozen large ships, more than one hundred schooners, and a thriving import and export business that covered the entire North American eastern sea coast as well as many parts of Europe. He was, however, no friend of the whale. A good part of his profits came from the sale of sperm oil candles, a very popular lighting device at the time.

The Revolutionary War brought an end to Lopez's high-riding fortunes at the same time as the conflict shattered Newport's economy. During the war, the British invaded and occupied the town. Because he had backed the patriot cause, the British seized Lopez's fleet of ships and nearly bankrupted him. To escape the British occupation, Lopez and other prominent Newport Jews fled north to Massachusetts, where they founded a Jewish community in Leicester.

After the war, Newport ceased to be a major commercial center. Boston and New York dominated the sea trade, but the postwar period also brought commercial troubles to many Jewish merchants in those towns. The continued conflict with the British after the Revolution made business in international trade decline drastically, and a sizable number of Jews had depended on the import and export business. It is estimated that the value of goods shipped back and forth across the

Atlantic dropped from a prewar high of about $60 million to less than $10 million by the time the War of 1812 was over.

This shift in the commercial trade winds wasn't the only new development North American Jews would have to cope with during the postwar years. Up until then, the vast majority of Jewish immigrants had been Sephardi Jews from Spain and Portugal, but as the 1800s continued, these Jews would be overwhelmed by a new wave of immigration of Ashkenazi Jews. These newly arrived Ashkenazi Jews didn't share all of the religious values and beliefs of the more well-established Jews of North America. The conflicts and accommodations between these two groups would give a new face to Judaism. It also would give birth to some of the most dynamic and vital Jewish communities in the world.

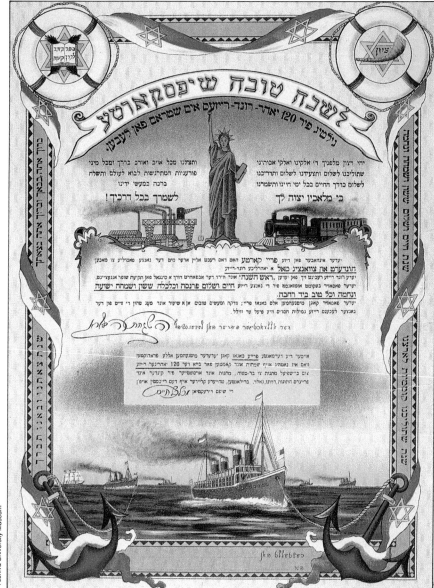

Yeshiva University Museum

The images on this New Year's card from the early 1900s—the Statue of Liberty, boats carrying immigrants, American factories, and steam engines—vividly express the faith of many Jewish newcomers that North America was the "Land of Opportunity."

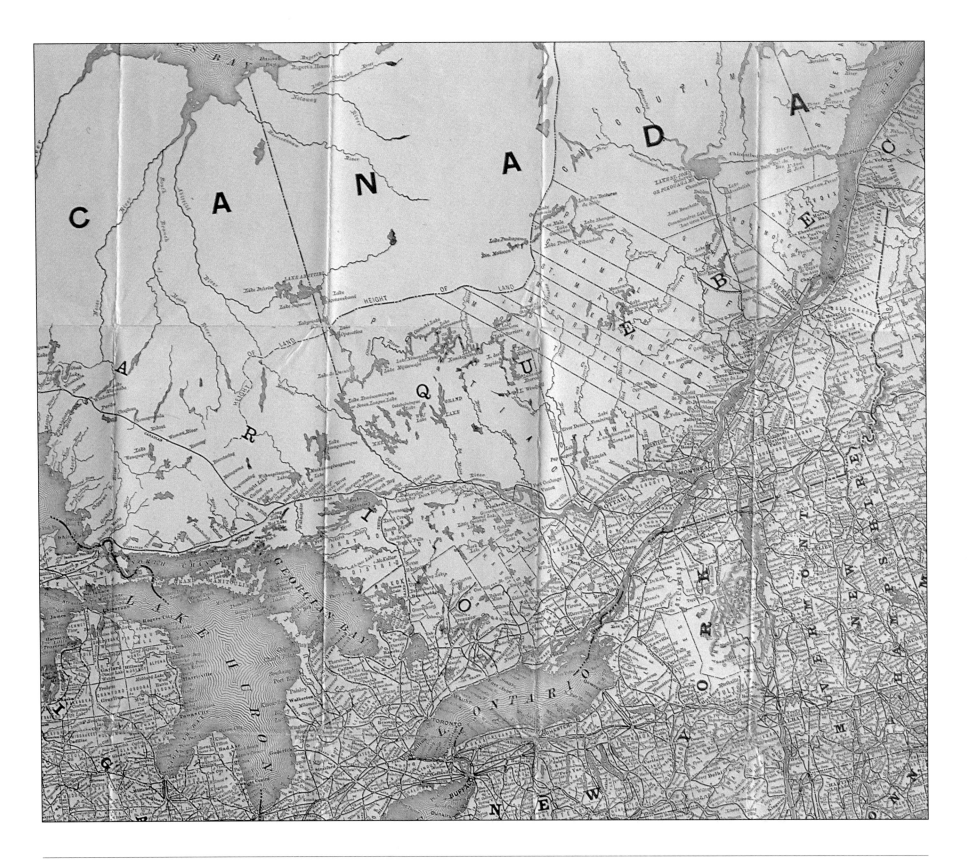

CHAPTER TWO:

American Jews Expand Their Horizons

U.S. and Canada Grow and New Jewish Communities Are Born

After the Revolution, the United States' international trade suffered badly, as did the fortunes of the Jews who were involved in commerce. A series of trade embargoes against England, the loss of status as a trading member of the British empire, and finally the War of 1812 between the United States and Britain curtailed most of the import and export business.

At this time, most North Americans were farmers, but the Jews living in the New World did not turn to this profession in very great numbers. Instead, many of them focused on the fur trade, which was still lucrative. Others became retailers. Those with money bought and sold real estate.

Many of the retailers started as peddlers. Settlements were spreading over the vast continent, and everywhere the settlers went, Jewish peddlers followed. As a matter of fact, Jewish peddlers became so ubiquitous on the frontier that the image of the Jew traveling door-to-door with an array of household goods soon became an accepted cliché.

As the United States and Canada grew, it was the Ashkenazi Jews who tended to move west from the eastern cities. The Sephardi families, who had been settled longer and were better established, remained for the most part along the Atlantic coast.

© Robert Kern

The Cincinnati Historical Society

Early in the nineteenth century, the widely scattered pioneers quickly coalesced into established settlements. Some Jews who moved into these new towns lost their Jewish identities. As they took on the characteristics of the other inhabitants and neglected their religion, they became indistinguishable from any of the other settlers.

Others persisted in retaining their ethnic identity. When Joseph Jonas moved to the frontier wilds of Ohio in 1817, he talked his two brothers as well as two other Jewish men into joining him. Once settled in Cincinnati, the five of them got together every Friday night and worshiped with whatever prayers and songs they could remember, ignoring the fact that Jewish law required a minimum of ten Jewish men, a minyan, for a formal religious service.

Seven years later, in 1824, enough Jews had moved into the frontier town of Cincinnati to make up a congregation: Bene Israel. At first, most of the Jews in the town had originally come from England. As long as the Jewish population consisted of immigrants with a homogenous British background, congregational politics proceeded smoothly. However, less than twenty years later, in 1840, so many German Jews had migrated to the area that they made up a majority of the Jewish community.

The German Jewish immigrants had serious differences with their English counterparts over what should and shouldn't be included in religious services. The more progressive German Jews generally believed in "reforming" the service, which meant such things as praying in unison, translating some of the prayers into English, and adding music to the service. Traditionally, none of these things had taken place at synagogue services. The more conservative Jews of British background were horrified at the proposed changes and fought them. Consequently, the German Jews broke away and formed their own temple: B'nai Jeshurun.

This split in Cincinnati mirrored the changes that were occurring across the continent in most Jewish communities. Floods of new immigrants as well as an industrialized economy and the settling of the West were radically changing the societies of both the United States and Canada. The insulated rural communities of pre-Revolutionary times were being eclipsed by cosmopolitan cities. By 1820, even Cincinnati had forty thousand inhabitants.

As a result, new ideas of how Jews could live their lives and what they should include in their rituals and beliefs were transforming individuals and society. Religious services weren't the only areas of Jewish life being reformulated: No longer were Jewish success stories simply tales of traders and merchants. Now Jews were beginning to take their place at the forefront of social thinking, government, journalism, and literature.

In many communities across North America, small groups of Jewish settlers worshiped in synagogues like the one pictured above in New Jersey. When Joseph Jonas (left) moved to Cincinnati in 1817, he was the city's only Jewish citizen.

The First Jewish Commodore

Take the case of Uriah Phillips Levy, who had a career that most eighteenth-century Jews probably would have thought impossible. Born in Philadelphia in 1792, he went to sea as a cabin boy at age ten. By the time he was in his twenties, he was a schooner captain. Never an easy man to get along with, Levy was removed from his schooner, the *George Washington,* by mutineers and left on a remote island. A tenacious opponent of anyone who crossed him, Levy returned to the United States and brought the mutineers to court. He won his case.

Levy enlisted in the U.S. Navy during the War of 1812. Although he was appointed a sailing master, Levy was not a typical ship's master. To observe the Jewish Sabbath, he confined himself to quarters every Saturday except for emergencies or if a battle was in the offing.

After capturing several British ships, Levy himself was captured and spent much of the war in a British prison camp. But even after he was released and back in the U.S. Navy once the war had ended, Levy did not have an easy time of it. Other Navy officers looked down on the proud man. They considered him common because he had risen from the ranks to his command while they had been born into upper-class families. Many of them were anti-Semitic and considered Jews to be their inferiors.

Levy brooked no trifling with his feelings or his career. Subsequently, he was court-martialed six times and kicked out of the Navy twice for dueling and insubordination. (In at least one duel, he killed another officer for making anti-Semitic remarks.) As he pointed out in a description of his life, "I was forced to encounter a large share of the prejudices and hostility by which, for so many ages, the Jew has been pursued."

Levy also made many enemies in the U.S. Navy because he was opposed to the corporal punishment of sailors, a common practice at the time. He would allow no flogging on ships under his command. The more conservative Navy brass considered flogging to be a necessary disciplinary tool.

In the end, Levy prevailed on the issue of corporal punishment. In 1855, after being demoted, he managed to have a special Congressional court of inquiry look into the specifics of the charges against him. He was exonerated of all wrongdoing. Subsequently, he was promoted to the post of commodore.

Eventually, Congress also went along with him in banning flogging and passed regulations outlawing the practice. This was Levy's proudest accomplishment. He said he wished to be remembered as the "father of the law for the abolition of the barbarous practice of corporal punishment in the Navy of the United States."

Levy didn't do so badly as a businessman, either. He made a fortune buying and selling New York City real estate. A great admirer of Thomas Jefferson, as a private citizen Levy purchased Monticello, Jefferson's home in Virginia, for a mere $2,700.

American Jewish Historical Society

Uriah Phillips Levy, who served as a commodore in the United States Navy, was instrumental in ending the barbaric practice of punishing sailors with floggings.

Sir   Monticello May 28.18.

I thank you for the Discourse on the consecration of the Synagogue in your city, with which you have been pleased to favor me. I have read it with pleasure and instruction, having learnt from it some valuable facts in Jewish history which I did not know before. your sect by it's sufferings has furnished a remarkable proof of the universal spirit of religious intolerance, inherent in every sect, disclaimed by all while feeble, and practised by all when in power. our laws have applied the only antidote to this vice, protecting our religious, as they do our civil rights by putting all on an equal footing. but more remains to be done. for altho' we are free by the law, we are not so in practice. public opinion erects itself into an Inquisition, and exercises it's office with as much fanaticism as fans the flames of an Auto da fé. the prejudice still scowling on your section of our religion, altho' the elder one, cannot be unfelt by yourselves. it is to be hoped that individual dispositions will at length mould themselves to the model of the law, and consider the moral basis on which all our religions rest, as the rallying point which unites them in a common interest; while the peculiar dogmas branching from it are the exclusive concern of the respective sects embracing them, and no rightful subject of notice to any other. public opinion needs reformation on this point, which would have the further happy effect of doing away the hypocritical maxim of 'intus ut lubet, foris ut moris.' nothing I think would be so likely to effect this as to your sect particularly as the more careful attention to education, which you recommend, and which placing it's members on the equal and commanding benches of science, will exhibit them as equal objects of respect and favor. I should not do full justice to the merits of your discourse, were I not, in addition to that of it's matter, to express my consideration of it as a fine specimen of style & composition. I salute you with great respect and esteem.

                                    Th.Jefferson

This letter from Thomas Jefferson to Mordecai Manuel Noah (above) acknowledges Noah's "discourse on the consecration of the synagogue in your city." Apparently Noah had written to Jefferson decrying the practice of anti-Semitism and Jefferson expressed gratitude for being informed of "some valuable facts in Jewish history."

At the time, the mansion was unwanted and falling apart. He renovated and restored Monticello to the condition it had been in when Jefferson lived there.

Levy also commissioned and donated the statue of Jefferson that stands in the Capitol in Washington, D.C. When Levy died, he left a very unusual will and a very unhappy widow. He stipulated that Monticello be left to the U.S. government, to be used for an agricultural institute. However, the family contested the will and won back the estate. In 1923, one of Levy's descendants sold it for $500,000.

A New Noah

Another forward-looking Jewish native of Philadelphia was Mordecai Manuel Noah, who was born in 1785, seven years before Commodore Levy. A journalist, politician, judge, law-enforcement officer, and playwright, Noah enjoyed a wide range of careers and made enough money to indulge in some of his more radical social ideas.

During the War of 1812, Noah was appointed consul to Tunisia, where he negotiated the release of hostages who had been taken by Tunisian pirates. Not very popular with the Washington establishment, his political enemies, some claim, had him removed from this post because he was Jewish.

After coming back to the United States, Noah moved to New York, where he became a self-styled spokesman for U.S. Jews. "…My own government insults the religious feelings of a whole nation [the Jews]," he said in connection with his recall from Tunis.

In New York, his political connections with Tammany Hall secured him a long list of jobs—including sheriff and port surveyor. He also found time to edit such newspapers as the New York *Enquirer,* the *Evening Star,* and the *National Advocate* (not all at the same time). He founded a weekly paper called the *Sunday Times and Messenger.* In between these tasks, he wrote plays.

Besides his indefatigable energy, Noah also possessed delusions of grandeur. He considered himself a divinely appointed Jewish leader with superior insight into the future of the Jewish people.

In 1825, Noah decided that Grand Island, a piece of land he had access to in the Niagara River near Buffalo, New York, could serve as the new homeland for the Jews until Palestine became available. He renamed the island Ararat, after the island where the biblical Noah had disembarked after the cessation of the great flood.

Along with Jews, Noah invited Amerindians to live on Ararat. He believed them to be the lost ten tribes of Israel—Jews who had been separated from other Jews during biblical times.

A master of publicity, Noah played up his idea with big headlines in the newspapers he edited. Then on September 15, 1825, he presided over the Ararat dedi-

Yeshiva University Museum

cation ceremonies, an event attended by local officials as well as the governor of New York.

In modern times, this would have been a great photo opportunity. Noah showed up in royal silk and ermine robes. Dedication ceremonies to standing-room-only crowds of curious citizens took place in the Episcopal Church of St. Paul in Buffalo. Bands played. Guns roared in salute. At the center of the proceedings, Noah presented a huge cornerstone dedicating "Ararat, a City of Refuge for the Jews, Founded by Mordecai Manuel Noah, in the [Jewish] month of Tizri, 5586 [the year according to the Jewish calendar], Sept 1825 & in the 50th year of American Independence." Then he gave a rather disjointed speech demonstrating how the island of Ararat would change the future history of the world.

Was Noah a fool, a con man, or a visionary? Whatever the answer, he certainly took himself seriously. The rest of the world, alas, was not so impressed. Jews never lived on his Grand Island, nor did the Amerindians. Still, some call him one of the first Zionists, since he advocated the Jewish return to Palestine. And you can still take a look at his beloved cornerstone. It's behind glass in the Buffalo Historical Museum.

He later encouraged Jews to purchase Palestine from the Turks so that all oppressed Jews could settle there. Unfortunately, he was 120 years ahead of history, and his treatise on the idea, "Discourse on the Restoration of the Jews," was negatively received, because it called on Christians for help and would have made the new nation too dependent on Europe.

But the most important lesson contained in Mordecai Noah's story is the fact that Jews were beginning to do some radical rethinking about themselves and Judaism. As their numbers grew, the Jews of North America began to develop new ideas about what it meant to be Jewish. New kinds of Jewish communities and religious organizations as well as Jewish life-styles would spring from these new concepts.

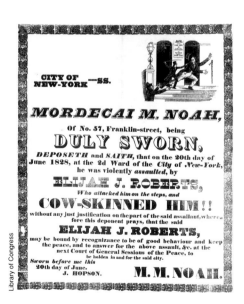

Mordecai Manuel Noah (above) espoused many controversial causes and led a colorful and eventful life. A document in which Noah accuses a business associate of assault (left) "without any just justification," is typical of the overblown rhetoric that characterized his diatribes.

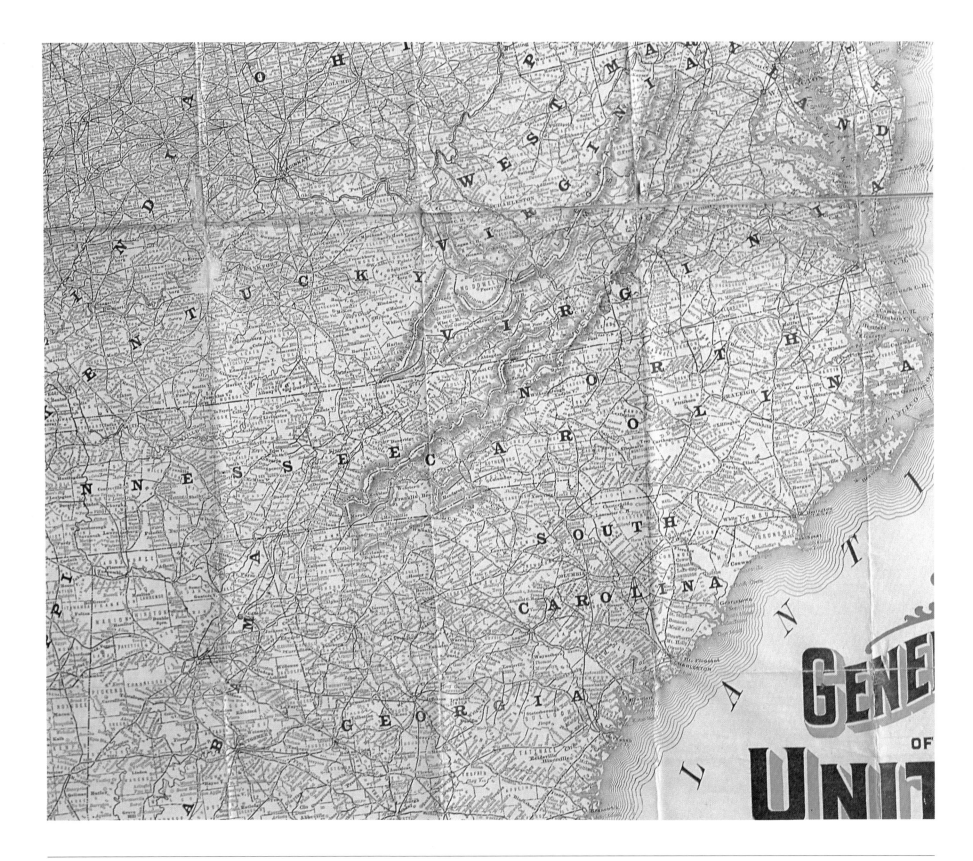

CHAPTER THREE:

Judaism in the New World Reforms

Looking back at Jewish history in North America, it seems inevitable that the interaction of Jews with different backgrounds from many different parts of the world would radically change the face of Judaism in the New World. On this continent there was too much freedom, too much room for the coexistence and intermingling of different concepts of what it means to be Jewish for there to be any other result.

One of the first signs of what was to come in the changing nature of Judaism was a sequence of events in Charleston, South Carolina, in the early 1800s.

At the time, Charleston was home to one of the most important and influential American Jewish communities. Early in the history of the colonies, this area had attracted Jewish settlers because of its forward-looking colonial charter. This document, drawn up by the liberal-minded English statesman and philosopher John Locke, guaranteed freedom to everyone who settled in the area, no matter what their religion. (This freedom, however, only applied to whites. It did not extend to African-Americans, for despite its liberality toward white minority groups, Charleston was a center for the slave trade. Similarly, Amerindians, while not enslaved, were prohibited from being citizens.)

While the Anglican residents of Charleston may not have been as liberal-minded as Locke in welcoming "Jews, heathens, and dissenters," they went along with the charter in order to attract more residents, because the land around Charleston was a swampy wilderness and it was hard to convince settlers to move in. The first Jews arrived in Charleston during the 1690s. In 1740, the Jewish community officially formed its first congregation—the third Jewish congregation in the colonies. In 1749, the first synagogue in Charleston was built.

By the 1820s, the Charleston congregation, Kahal Kadosh Beth Elohim, was the largest congregation in the United States. It was also the wealthiest. But while it was successful in numbers and finances, revolt was brewing among its members. The congregation had originally consisted of Sephardi Jews, but it had grown to include many Ashkenazi Jews, many of them from Germany, and the religious services, while still following the basic structure of Sephardic services, had acquired many Ashkenazic characteristics.

As a result, the religious services had become quite chaotic. Custom called for a long Friday-night service lasting up to three hours. For most of the service, worshipers were largely on their own, reciting Hebrew prayers at whatever speed

By the second decade of the nineteenth century, Charleston, South Carolina (below), was home to the largest Jewish congregation in the United States.

American Jewish Archives

they wished. What upset some congregants, however, was the coming and going of worshipers who disregarded the prayers. The roiling anarchy inside the temple was exacerbated by people who conversed, laughed, paid infrequent attention to the services, and continually entered and exited.

Another practice that annoyed some congregants was a fund-raising ploy: If you wanted to say the blessing over the Torah, you had to pay for the honor.

One of the dissatisfied temple members was a man named Isaac Harby, a journalist, novelist, and teacher who was born in 1788. In 1824, Harby drew up a petition demanding that Beth Elohim's temple services embody a "more respectable state of discipline."

The Beth Elohim synagogue in Charleston was the site of early conflicts between what would become Orthodox and Reform Jewish beliefs.

American Jewish Archives

After Beth Elohim in Charleston was destroyed by fire in the 1830s, the congregation replaced it with a building that included an organ.

Harby's petition contained some ideas considered radical in these early days. He wanted some of the service to be read in English so that congregants would know what the prayers meant, so they could grasp its "beauty and meaning." He also wanted services to be shorter. He wanted to stop repeating some of the prayers in Spanish, a holdover from when most of the congregants spoke Spanish. He also asked that the trustees of Beth Elohim stop selling prayers and support the temple solely on membership subscriptions.

The petition, signed by Harby and forty-six other temple members, was rejected by the trustees. So twelve of the petitioners, including Harby, broke away and formed their own organization, called the Reformed Society of Israelites.

Although relatively short-lived, the Reformed Society of Israelites is generally credited with being the first "Reform" temple in North America. The older institution was labeled "Orthodox."

Lacking a rabbi, the society held its own services led by lay members of its congregation. They wrote and distributed their own prayer book, used organ music during services, did away with requiring head coverings for male worshipers, and drew up ten articles of faith that tried not to "restrict the faith or conscience of any man."

Although Harby saw his efforts at Jewish reform as parallel to those Luther had brought to Christianity, he did not possess the charisma, intellectual skills, or the social power to create a large movement on his own. After eight years, the Reformed Society of Israelites disbanded. Harby, broke and disillusioned when his reform movement fizzled, died in New York in 1828 at age forty. He didn't know that a Jewish reform movement would soon surge across the continent—and across the world.

Even though Harby's ideas had not given birth to an overwhelming reform movement, they did cause significant ripples in North American Jewish life. Jews in the major cities argued over the Charleston articles of faith. Debates raged over the acceptability of praying to God in English rather than exclusively worshiping in Hebrew.

The new concepts gradually held sway over many Jews. Within twenty years of Harby's death, there were at least ten Orthodox temples that had introduced modest reforms to their services. And there were three temples on the East Coast that had wholeheartedly adopted the concept of reform.

Ironically, the first temple to embrace enthusiastically most of Harby's reform ideas turned out to be Charleston's Beth Elohim—the very congregation that had shown Harby the door when he had demanded changes.

In 1836, Gustavus Poznanski, who had been born in Poland in 1805, was appointed rabbi of Beth Elohim. He had been the lay leader of the Shearith Israel congregation in New York since 1832. By offering him more money and the title of rabbi, the Charleston group lured him to the South.

Poznanski had spent time in Hamburg, Germany, the center of the European Jewish reform movement, so he was familiar with the principles of reform. As leader of Beth Elohim, he succeeded where Harby had failed. He gradually introduced modernizing changes that mirrored Harby's concepts. Prayers were read in English as well as in Hebrew. Services were no longer anarchic and noisy; they were disciplined and orderly and dignified. Poznanski delivered his sermons in English.

And when Beth Elohim's original temple burned down in 1838, thirty-eight parishioners signed a new petition requesting that the new building include an organ "to assist in the vocal parts of the services." It was done. When the new temple was completed in 1840, the drifting tones of an organ accompanied services in the congregation's new home.

This plaque celebrates the ministry of Gustavus Poznanski who helped pioneer Reform Judaism in the United States.

New York Public Library

After assuming his rabbinical post at B'nai Jeshurun in Cincinnati (opposite), Isaac Mayer Wise (above) became a forceful crusader for Reform Judaism throughout North America.

The Reform Movement Gains Strength

Still, the reform movement did not become a force to be reckoned with until Isaac Mayer Wise, a rabbi from Bohemia, arrived to give it strong leadership and direction. Born in 1819, Wise claimed to have been ordained as a rabbi in Prague in 1842 at twenty-three, and he said he was forced to leave Europe because of conflict with the Imperial Council of Prague. Wise said they had wanted to limit the number of Jewish marriages and he had refused.

Historians dispute Wise's version of his early life, however, claiming there are no records showing he ever attended the University of Prague or was ordained in Prague.

Whatever the truth about Wise's early years, as soon as he arrived in New York, his friends told him to forget about being an American rabbi. In America, they said, there was no money or status in it. He'd be better off hitting the road as a peddler.

Instead, Wise opened a basement language school where he taught new Jewish immigrants how to speak, read, and write English. Eventually, he applied for a rabbinical post at the Beth El Temple in Albany, New York. After a brief Albany audition in which he delivered a sample sermon, he was offered the job. Reportedly, one of the Beth El members told him that the temple members "liked and admired you...because they don't understand you."

When they finally did understand him, some of the congregants intensely disliked what they were hearing. Wise openly admitted that he didn't believe in the coming of a Messiah, a belief that many Jews hold sacred. He had the men and women sit together in the temple. This new arrangement alienated some members of the congregation—traditionally, women sat in their own section of the temple. Wise also integrated the choir so that it included women, and he advocated advanced education for the female children of the congregants.

All of these factors led to a serious rift between the more conservative members of Beth El, led by the temple president Louis Spanier, and the reform-minded Jews who looked to Wise for leadership. Albany's Orthodox Jewish community was so offended that they excommunicated Wise. Spanier tried to oust him, but Wise resisted efforts to make him leave.

Events reached a climax on the holiday of Rosh Hashanah in 1849. During services, Spanier punched Wise in the nose. A minor riot ensued, with the younger members of the congregation—who supported Wise—battling the older members. The fighting spilled out into the street, where the sheriff and police broke up the melee.

Wise claimed that he'd file a civil suit and take Spanier to court. Spanier replied that he had enough money to countersue and ruin the rabbi. Eventually, Spanier had to pay a fine, and Wise left Beth El for another, smaller Albany temple.

Synagogue B'nai Jeshurun gave Isaac M. Wise a forum for promoting Reform Judaism.

Wise wasn't happy in his new pulpit. He considered himself a star in the reform movement and wasn't content with a small congregation in upstate New York. For a time, he considered an offer from Charleston to be the rabbi at Beth Elohim. At first he agreed to take this job, but then he changed his mind. Although it is not clear why, he couldn't see a real opportunity to make his mark there either. Some historians believe he refused this post because he didn't want to follow in the footsteps of Rabbi Poznanski, who had already made big waves in Charleston.

Then, in 1854, Temple B'nai Jeshurun in Cincinnati, Ohio, made him an offer of a rabbinical post he didn't refuse. He decided that the Midwest was where he would play his part. And sure enough, as a rabbi in Cincinnati, he had a starring role in the nineteenth-century progress of Reform Judaism.

As Wise accepted his new position, a three-way battle for the hearts and minds of North American Jews was taking shape. The Orthodox Jews believed that no change in services or beliefs was to be allowed. All prayers were to be in Hebrew. A central tenet was the belief in the future coming of the Messiah, who would save the world. Friday-night services had to be held as soon as the sun went down. No Jew was allowed to work, ride in a wagon, or light fires of any kind after sundown on Friday until sundown on Saturday. Men and women sat separately at religious services, and at those services, all men wore hats.

Isaac Mayer Wise poses for a bust at Hebrew Union College.

At the other extreme were radical Reform rabbis, many of whom had immigrated from Germany. They believed in secularizing Judaism—making it more mainstream and less distinguishable from Christian life. Some believed that the Jewish Sabbath should be moved from Saturday to Sunday. Some advocated scrapping all of the Hebrew prayers and praying completely in English. Others substituted modern poetry for traditional hymns.

One radical society, the New York Society for Ethical Culture, accepted both Jews and non-Jews in their "congregation." This society was open to all who rejected biblical teachings for a modern philosophical approach to ethical behavior. In one of their departures from traditional Jewish practices, the society substituted poetry by Robert Browning for the Kaddish, the traditional prayer for the dead.

In this chaotic scenario that threatened to fragment North American Jews into myriad warring factions, Wise saw his proselytizing opportunity. If he could work out a compromise platform between Orthodox and Reform extremes, a platform of beliefs and practices that would attract a substantial number of North American Jews, then New World Judaism could consolidate itself into an important force in modern life. Such a movement would have to integrate itself into modern society while maintaining its Jewish identity—but the changes would have to be moderate. It was evident that the more radical reformers were introducing so many secularizing changes that their Jewish identity was threatened.

In Cincinnati, Wise made the same changes he had made in Albany. Organ music was played at services and families could sit together. Women weren't banished to a separate section of the temple. Men didn't have to wear hats. And Wise delivered his sermons in English while urging other rabbis to follow suit.

Curiously enough, while the original Sephardi Jews had insisted on sermons in Spanish in the 1850s, many rabbis considered it essential to give their sermons in their native tongue of German. Wise believed that it was time to start talking in the North American vernacular. Using English would help put Judaism into the mainstream of North American life.

Wise also instituted other changes designed to increase attendance at religious services and make Judaism more amenable to the North American way of life without diluting Jewish ethnic identity. Instead of holding Friday-night services right after sundown, he moved them to a later time, making it easier for congregants to attend after work.

He also recognized that the custom of not riding wagons on Saturday was unrealistic in North America. While European Jews may have lived in close quarters and not found it inconvenient to walk to Saturday's Sabbath services, North Americans lived much farther apart. It was unrealistic to ask them to walk miles to services. So instead of prohibiting the riding of wagons on the Sabbath, he preached that it was virtuous to take a wagon to temple.

Wise didn't just practice and preach these ideas to his own congregation, he took his show on the road, too. For the next fifty years, he spoke to any group that

Hebrew Union College, which Isaac Mayer Wise helped found, has been an important institution for training Reform rabbis who have served the Jewish congregations of North America.

The Cincinnati Historical Society

would have him. He published his ideas in both English and German. He also pushed for a national organization of Reform congregations. He believed that such an organization would enable him to put his indelible stamp on North American Judaism. As a step toward that unification, he published the *Minhag America,* a prayer book that incorporated prayers in both Hebrew and English (there was also a version that combined German with Hebrew). The book came out in 1857 and was sold to congregations and individuals across the continent. Sixteen years later, in 1873, his vision of a North American Jewish organization came true. That year, thirty-four congregations sent representatives to the first meeting of the Union of American Hebrew Congregations.

Wise also pushed for a national school for the study of Judaism. In general, the issue of establishing advanced schools that could ordain rabbis long had been a thorny problem for North American Jews. While a few had gone to sectarian or Christian colleges, many of these schools would either not let Jews matriculate or enforced draconian quota systems that severely limited the number of Jewish students. In addition, all attempts at establishing advanced schools foundered because of lack of students and money. Virtually all of the North American rabbis had been trained in Europe. During the 1850s, Wise himself had briefly run a school called Zion College, but it only attracted about a dozen students, and like all the other attempts before it, it quickly closed its doors.

By the 1870s, the reform movement, largely through Wise's efforts, had attracted enough attention and enthusiasm to support a full-time college. Henry Adler, a benefactor from Indiana, donated $10,000 for the establishment of a Jewish rabbinical school. With this money and other contributions, Wise opened the Hebrew Union College in Cincinnati in 1875. In the beginning, the school had only thirteen students (one of whom was an eleven-year-old girl).

At this time, North American rabbis also did not command much respect or salary, so students had to be culled from the poor and desperate. Nine of Hebrew Union College's first thirteen students dropped out, including the young girl, but the four who did graduate went on to become the distinguished heads of Reform congregations.

The acceptance of women at Union College was an advanced notion at the time. Few people believed that women were capable of going to college. Most of those who did believe women could go on to higher learning advocated the establishment of separate women's colleges.

Although Union College may have accepted women, that didn't mean, however, that any graduated. Apparently, the idea of female rabbis in the nineteenth century was too radical even for the reformers. One historian claims that the college administrators made sure that none of the female students completed their studies by making sure they all got married while they were still undergraduates —thereby avoiding the issue of ordaining women. As a result, no women were ordained until 1972.

The Cincinnati Historical Society

Hebrew Union College in Cincinnati began with one building and thirteen students in 1875.

Orthodox Battles Reform

As the 1880s began, all of Wise's efforts at establishing a reform movement seemed to be overwhelmingly successful. Most of the Jews in the United States at this time were now of German origin—it is estimated that they numbered more than two hundred and fifty thousand, while the population of Sephardi Jews stayed at around fifty thousand. A large majority of these German immigrants or families of German origin belonged to Reform congregations.

While the Sephardic congregations had been predominant in terms of money and numbers when North America was a rural backwater, once the United States and Canada started to become industrialized international powers, Reform German Jews stepped up to the vanguard of Jewish culture and theology.

Just when it seemed that the Orthodox wing of North American Judaism had about passed from the scene, however, two events came storming over the historical horizon to revive the movement, boost its morale, and give it a new sense of purpose.

What set the scene for the revival of the Orthodox movement was a character-istic that had always been Reform's weak spot: the constant tendency to weaken its Jewish identity as it compromised with modern society in its efforts to keep Jews in the fold. While Wise had skillfully modernized and adapted Judaism to the North American way of life while still holding on to its ethnic integrity, his Orthodox opponents were always on the lookout for areas where Wise and his colleagues could be attacked for having gone too far over the line toward secular concerns.

Curiously enough, it was a banquet in Cincinnati, in 1883, that afforded the Orthodox factions their first significant opportunity in decades to strike back at the Reformers. The feast was held to celebrate the tenth anniversary of the Union of American Hebrew Congregations. As a conciliatory gesture, Wise even invited Orthodox rabbis to the meal. Many believe that in the back of Wise's mind, he still held out hope that the Orthodox rabbis would give in eventually to some of his concepts and join the reform movement in some way or other.

Instead, the event inflamed the Orthodox attendees. As can happen at such large events, the caterer didn't get the menu right. Presumably, there were no Jewish caterers in Cincinnati at that time who were capable of feeding such a large crowd, so a gentile caterer was hired. Someone allegedly explained to the caterer how a kosher meal—one prepared according to Jewish dietary rules—should be served, but it wasn't explained very well. And, certainly, no one examined the food before it was served to the more than two hundred distinguished rabbis from across the continent.

The first course was clams, a shocking choice. The consumption of shellfish is forbidden by Jewish dietary laws. Next came crabs and shrimp, two more forbidden foods. The main course included frogs' legs, which is also *treif*—nonkosher and forbidden.

The Orthodox rabbis stormed out in a rage at this insufferable insult to their palates. And in the days, weeks, and months that followed, their rage fueled the moribund Orthodox movement. For a solid year, headlines appeared in Orthodox publications about the horrors of the Cincinnati banquet and the anathema that was Reform Judaism. Article after article denounced Wise and his radicals and attacked the Hebrew Union College along with everything connected with it. For twelve months, the vitriolic editorials flowed in a rapacious storm of denunciations.

Then, just when the uproar over the infamous banquet quieted down, the Reform movement experienced another setback. This time, the disaster took the form of a list of principles called the Pittsburgh Platform, which can be viewed as an extension of Wise's famous belief that Judaism should be on the watch for "whatever makes us ridiculous before the world as it now is, [for these customs] may safely and should be abolished."

The Pittsburgh Platform, however, went too far in repudiating longstanding Jewish belief and stirred up Orthodox ire. Drawn up by one of the reform movement's intellectual stars, Kaufmann Kohler, the platform was designed as a rebuttal to the attacks of Alexander Kohut, Kohler's main Orthodox opponent.

These two rabbinical rivals—Kohut, who was born in 1842 in Hungary, and Kohler, who had been born the year before in Germany—had both been educated in Europe before immigrating to the United States. Once in the New World, each acted as a vociferous spokesman for his brand of Judaism: Kohut for Orthodox, Kohler for Reform.

Kohut, a formidable scholar, did not have any formal schooling until he was nearly eight years old. He was born into an impoverished family living in rural Hungary where education was unavailable. But after being snatched by gypsies (for his good looks, it was said) and then rescued by his family, he was moved to a more

Das Highland Haus, a catering hall in Cincinnati, was the scene of a disastrous banquet at which Orthodox rabbis were scandalized at being served nonkosher foods. Originally intended to improve relations between the American Jewish Reform movement and Orthodox Jews, the 1883 meeting inflamed them instead.

American Jewish Archives

urban area and put in school. He soon displayed outstanding academic talent.

While in Europe, Kohut churned out an eight-volume study of the Talmud, the set of traditional Jewish laws. (These eight volumes are still read by many Jews today.) At the peak of his Hungarian career, Kohut was appointed the superintendent of Hungary's school system, sat in Hungary's parliament as the Jewish representative, and continually delivered sparkling lectures attended by dignitaries and intellectuals. He was a star, but like many European luminaries, he was fated to come to North America where the audiences were larger and richer.

American Orthodox Jews lured Kohut to North America with promises of money and power. He arrived in New York in 1885 as the chief rabbi of Ahavath Chesed in New York City, perhaps the top Orthodox post in the country at the time. He was soon giving thunderous anti-Reform lectures, which he named after a section of the Talmud—"The Ethics of Our Fathers."

Kohler, the Reform scholar who stood up to Kohut's vociferous attacks, also had an impressive résumé that included some of Europe's top academic institutions in such cities as Munich, Berlin, and Leipzig. He came to the United States in 1869 and led a congregation in Detroit. Two years later, he moved to Chicago where he was the rabbi of the Sinai Congregation. Here he gave Sunday lectures as well as sermons on Saturday.

It was generally felt that in the nineteenth-century debate between Orthodox and Reform ideas, Kohut ran circles around Kohler. The Pittsburgh Platform was an effort by Kohler and Wise to fire an intellectual blast at Kohut that he couldn't recover from. Instead, the salvo missed its mark and hobbled its originators.

In 1885, Kohler chaired the meeting of nineteen delegates from Reform congregations across the continent who formally drew up the document. It called for abandoning the notion that the Bible was a divinely written book. It called for abandoning the kosher dietary laws. It called for abandoning Zionist efforts to settle Jews in the area known as Palestine. It called for abandoning Jewish hopes that a Messiah would come some day.

The Orthodox leaders viewed the Pittsburgh Platform as a new call to action. They argued that the platform was really calling for the abandonment of Judaism. What would remain if all these beliefs and customs were left behind? They believed that the reformers were emphasizing the negative and neglecting the positive. "Look at all they are against!" they shouted. "But what are they for?" The resulting tumult had the opposite effect than Kohler intended: the Orthodox movement was given new intellectual and spiritual impetus.

What neither the German Orthodox nor the German Reform Jews realized in 1885, however, was that American Judaism was headed for even more radical changes. In the same manner that large numbers of immigrant German Jews had taken over the leadership of North American Judaism from the Sephardi Jews, overwhelming numbers of newly arrived Russian Jews were about to seize the mantle from German Jews.

American Jewish Archives

Alexander Kohut (above), a rabbi born in Hungary, was an important spokesperson for American Orthodox Jewry during the nineteenth century. Kaufmann Kohler (opposite), a Reform rabbi from Germany, headed the 1885 delegation that drew up the Pittsburgh Platform, an important statement of Reform doctrine.

Daniel Guggenheim helped expand his family's business into mining, creating one of the largest family fortunes in the world.

CHAPTER FOUR:

Nineteenth-Century Jewish Family Dynasties

While Wise and his fellow reformers were introducing a new type of Judaism to the world and arguing about what Judaism should contain, other German Jews who had moved to North America were concerning themselves with more secular pursuits. In their drive to succeed commercially and socially, some of these Jewish tycoons were establishing powerful family dynasties that still influence society today.

One of these families was the Gratz clan. Barnard Gratz had been born in Poland, settled briefly in England, and then had come to Philadelphia in 1754. His brother Michael, who had spent some time in India, joined him, and the two enjoyed huge success in banking, importing and exporting, and real estate. Soon they were selling supplies to the British during the French and Indian Wars. When the Revolution came, they supplied the American rebel armies. In 1782, Barnard Gratz laid the cornerstone for Philadelphia's first synagogue.

The Gratz family grew quickly in numbers and wealth. Michael had a dozen children. After graduating from the University of Pennsylvania, his son Benjamin was appointed an officer in the U.S. forces fighting the War of 1812. Benjamin later moved to Lexington, Kentucky, where he was one of the founders of the Lexington & Ohio Railroad and an owner of the Bank of Kentucky. One of his daughters married into the family of Henry Clay, one of Kentucky's most powerful politicians.

The Gratz family seemed destined to obtain wealth and influence. Hyman Gratz, another of Michael's offspring, stayed close to home in Philadelphia. He was influential in the Federalist party, a political party that molded the early national government of the United States. He helped found the Pennsylvania Academy of Fine Arts and worked as a director of the Pennsylvania Company for Life Insurance.

American Jewish Archives

American Jewish Archives

Hyman Gratz (above) was active in the Federalist party, a political group that influenced early American government. His brother, Michael (right), spent time in India before emigrating to the United States.

Delaware Art Museum

Rebecca Gratz, a renowned beauty and tireless champion of the poor and underprivileged, was the model for Sir Walter Scott's heroine in *Ivanhoe*.

Another son, Jacob, was president of the Union Canal Company as well as a powerful state legislator. And Michael's daughter Richea is believed to be the first Jewish woman to go to college in North America. She graduated from Marshall, a school in Lancaster, Pennsylvania.

But the immortal star of the family was Rebecca—intelligent, beautiful, and selfless. Artists came from everywhere to paint her portrait. She was good friends with the author of *The Legend of Sleepy Hollow,* Washington Irving. When Thomas Sully, the well-known early-American artist, came to town, Irving insisted that he paint Rebecca. Sully was easily persuaded since Rebecca was reputed to be the most beautiful woman in Philadelphia. Sully said she had "elegant bearing, a melodiously sympathetic voice, [and] a simple and frank and gracious womanliness." E.G. Malbone, another prominent painter, also painted her picture.

Physical beauty wasn't the only source of Rebecca's renown. When Irving's fiancée, Matilda Hoffman, fell ill with tuberculosis in 1809, Rebecca was at Matilda's side for the last six months of her life. Stricken with grief, Irving traveled to Europe for comfort. There he met Sir Walter Scott, who was planning his book *Ivanhoe.* Irving's description of Rebecca must have made a powerful impression on Scott; she became his model for the character of the tragic Jewess Rebecca in his novel. The virtuous Rebecca is at the center of the story. Afterward, Scott asked Irving, "Does the Rebecca I have pictured here compare well with the pattern given?"

Still, Rebecca Gratz's philanthropy would have the most far-reaching effect on American society, setting the tone for the Jewish philanthropic agencies that would follow. In 1801, she took the job as secretary of the first nonsectarian organization for helping the destitute of Philadelphia: The Female Association for the Relief of Women and Children in Reduced Circumstances.

Later on, she founded and served as secretary for the Philadelphia Orphan Asylum. She held this post for over forty years. And in 1819, she was instrumental in the establishment of the Female Hebrew Benevolent Society, an agency aimed at providing aid to indigent Jewish women. This was the first organized Jewish women's group in America, a forerunner of other similar organizations. Rebecca was also involved in the first North American Hebrew Sunday school, which was started in 1838. Never one for short residencies in her posts, she served as president of the school for twenty-six years, until she was eighty-three.

With all her wealth, fame, and beauty, Rebecca Gratz never married. It is said that the true love of her life was Samuel Ewing, the son of Dr. John Ewing, provost of the University of Pennsylvania. But unlike many Jews, who, then as now, married outside of their faith, Rebecca admitted "my most cherished friends have generally been worshipers of a different faith than mine," but she refused to consider marrying a Christian.

National Museum of American Jewish History

Rachel Gratz (above), Rebecca Gratz's niece, was the frequent subject of many early-American portraitists. This needlepoint sampler (opposite) was begun by Rebecca Gratz and finished by her niece Rachel.

His fortune grew. When he was approached by Charles Graham, a Pennsylvania Quaker, for money to finance a mine in Leadville, Colorado, Meyer bought an interest in the mine instead. It proved to be a prudent investment. Soon he was raking in millions of dollars from silver and lead, and he abandoned his other businesses to focus on mining.

In 1882, Meyer Guggenheim and his seven sons formed M. Guggenheim's Sons. Of Meyer's offspring, his son Daniel proved to be the best at running the mining operations. By the end of the 1880s, the firm was operating smelters in Colorado and Mexico. As the 1890s began, Meyer and his family moved from Philadelphia to New York City to be in the center of the financial action.

Toward the end of the nineteenth century, the Guggenheim mining operations were an international phenomenon. In South America, the family owned mines in Bolivia and Chile. In Africa, they ran mines in the Congo and Angola. Their workers took gold out of the ground in Alaska. They owned half of the world's copper resources. Their companies included the Mexican Esperanza Gold Mine, the Nevada Consolidated Company, and the Chile Copper Company as well as the Colorado Smelting and Refining Company.

As their operations increased, the Guggenheims moved into direct competition with other American capitalists in the battle to control the flow of metals and

ores. In the late 1890s, Adolph Lewisohn, the patriarch of another Jewish family with wide mining interests, entered into a venture with the Rockefellers that was designed to control and manipulate the mining and selling of important metals being produced in North America. The cartel, known as the American Smelting and Refining Company, was formed by buying up about two dozen mining and smelting firms and consolidating them into one giant firm, or trust. The Rockefellers and Lewisohns offered to let the Guggenheims in on the scheme, but the Guggenheims, under the leadership of Daniel and Meyer, decided not to take part. They had other plans.

Using classic monopoly tactics, the Guggenheims ran rings around the other company when they manipulated prices by dumping vast supplies of lead on the open market, forcing the prices down and forcing American Smelting to accept huge losses. When a miners' strike shut down a large part of American Smelting's operations, the Guggenheims exploited the company's labor problems by buying large amounts of the company's stock at low prices. When it was all over, the Guggenheims weren't just partners in American Smelting—they had taken it over. Daniel Guggenheim became president and four of his brothers were elected to the board of directors.

Meyer Guggenheim lived to be seventy-six and died in 1905. Aside from amassing riches, the family went on to donate large sums of money to charity and to build museums, most notably the Solomon R. Guggenheim Museum in New York City, a striking, circular structure devoted to modern art.

While there were a great many successful nineteenth-century German Jewish businessmen, there is one more family deserving of particular mention. In 1852, Lazarus Straus came to North America from Otterberg in Bavaria and settled in Talbotton, Georgia. In partnership with two of his three sons, Isidor and Nathan, Lazarus built a successful merchandising business. By the time of the Civil War, the family was well-known enough for Isidor to be selected as an agent for the Confederacy and travel to Europe in an effort to sell Confederate war bonds and buy military supplies for the Southern armies. But by the end of the war, Sherman's march through Georgia had devastated the family business.

Rather than try to rebuild their enterprise in Georgia, the Straus family wisely moved to New York City. They entered into a partnership with Rowland H. Macy to set up a department store. Eventually they bought Macy out and developed Macy's into the biggest store of its kind in the world. They had the foresight to move the store from New York's Fourteenth Street—which was then Manhattan's main commercial district—uptown to the more remote Herald Square. The move was wildly successful. Herald Square quickly grew and eclipsed Fourteenth Street as a center of business.

Isidor Straus and his wife died on the *Titanic*. Nathan went on to gain a reputation as a sharp business leader and renown as a generous philanthropist. In the hard winters during the 1890s, he gave away more than a million buckets of coal to

Courtesy of the Smithsonian Institution

Simon Guggenheim (opposite, top) started business in Pennsylvania as a peddler. His son Meyer (opposite, bottom, surrounded by his family in 1889) ensured the success of the family business when he developed a new formula for stove polish. Macy's (above), the world's biggest department store, was founded by Lazarus Straus (in partnership with R. H. Macy). Straus had moved to New York City from Atlanta because of the Civil War.

American Jewish Archives

When Adolph Ochs died, he left the *New York Times* to his daughter Iphigene Bertha Ochs.

the unemployed. He built lodging houses for the poor where they could sleep and eat for a nickel a day. He and his wife, Lina, were instrumental in forcing local governments to require the pasteurization of milk. (At the time, thousands of infants were dying from drinking contaminated milk.) Straus personally built and paid for pasteurization plants in more than thirty large cities. It is estimated that the pasteurization of milk cut the infant mortality rate in half.

Straus also donated money to help rebuild Palestine, including the Nathan and Lina Straus Health Centers located in Jerusalem and Tel Aviv. Straus ordered that the centers treat all who needed help regardless of religion or ethnic group.

Another one of Lazarus Straus' sons, Oscar Solomon Straus, went on to a successful career in politics. U.S. president Grover Cleveland appointed him ambassador to Turkey in 1887. In 1906, Theodore Roosevelt appointed him U.S. secretary of commerce and labor. In 1912, Oscar ran for the governor of New York and lost, but his books and speeches continued to be influential. After World War I, he took part in the peace conferences and warned of the continued dangers to Europe's minority ethnic groups. The Nazi outrages that followed two decades later proved him tragically correct.

The Ochs Family and North America's Most Influential Newspaper

In the U.S. media, four newspapers are generally accepted as being the most influential: the *New York Times*, the *Washington Post*, the *Los Angeles Times*, and the *Wall Street Journal*. Of these, the publication with the most clout is the *New York Times*. It is probably the most influential newspaper in the world, but it might not even exist today if it weren't for the Ochs family, German Jews who immigrated to the United States from Bavaria in 1845.

When he came to the United States from Europe, Julius Ochs did not settle down immediately. He went from job to job and from town to town in Kentucky and Tennessee. In Nashville, he married Bertha Levy, who had also come to North America from Bavaria.

Despite living in Tennessee and the fact that his wife's family were solidly on the side of the Confederacy, Julius Ochs fought for the Union Army during the Civil War. After Lee surrendered at Appomattox, Ochs moved his family to Knoxville, Tennessee. Despite the family's poverty, he served as a volunteer lay rabbi in the local congregation.

Because the family was so poor, Julius Ochs' son, Adolph, had to quit school at age eleven and go to work. It was while working as a teenager at the *Knoxville Chronicle* that Adolph became enamored of the newspaper business. (He later said that the "printing office was my high school and university.") He started as an office boy and then became what was known as a "printer's devil" in the production department. He was independent-minded and willing to take a risk. At nineteen, he moved to Chattanooga, Tennessee, where he bought the failing *Chattanooga Times* for a mere $250.

Ochs had a talent for running a paper. The teenager not only soon had the *Chattanooga Times* showing a profit, he also reshaped it into one of the Southern states' most important publications through the erudition of its editorials. His social connections improved, too. He married Effie Miriam Wise in 1883 when he was twenty-five. Wise was the daughter of Isaac Mayer Wise, the Cincinnati rabbi who was leading the American Jewish Reform movement.

In the 1890s, Ochs got wind of another paper that was teetering on the edge of failure: the *New York Times*. With its daily circulation barely over nine thousand, the paper was losing more than $300,000 a year and was about to go under. For $75,000, Ochs bought the *New York Times*. And there is no question it proved to be a great investment.

At the time, the competing New York dailies, the *New York World* and the *New York Journal,* were using lurid reports of crime and corruption and semifactual, sensational stories of sex and hanky-panky among the celebrities of the day to build readership. After he took over, Ochs banned "yellow" journalism (sensationalism) from the *Times*. He decided the paper would occupy a "clean, dignified, and trustworthy" journalistic niche.

To emphasize his squeaky-clean principles, he put the slogan "All the News That's Fit to Print" across the top of the paper. The inference was that if readers wanted "unfit" news, they would have to read one of the paper's competitors. One famous newsroom story claimed that when a *Times* city editor assigned a story on sexual molestation, he said, "Here's an incest story. Keep it clean."

Under Ochs' leadership, the paper went from its low point of a circulation of nine thousand to about five hundred thousand in 1935, the year Adolph Ochs died. After his death, his daughter, Iphigene Bertha Ochs, inherited the paper, and she ran it with her husband, Adolph Hays Sulzberger.

The New York Times

Julius Ochs, Adolph's father, upset his Tennessee in-laws by fighting for the Union in the Civil War.

The New-York Times.

CHAPTER FIVE

The Russian Jews Arrive

Pogroms in Russia Send Immigrants to North America

It is estimated that by 1880 there were about two hundred and fifty thousand Jews living in the United States. About a fifth of these were Sephardi Jews—originally from Spain and Portugal—and the rest were virtually all Ashkenazi Jews of German origin. But the situation was about to change drastically. Mainly because of violent anti-Semitic attacks engineered by the czar of Russia, the German Jews would soon be outnumbered by a tide of new immigrants from Eastern Europe.

Some historians believe that there were Jewish settlements in Russia even before the "Russians" arrived, but certainly the population grew after the Romans conquered Jerusalem around the time of Jesus and many Jews moved north. The Jews' longevity in Russia did not give them any real social power, any more than the Amerindians' long residence in North America gave them primacy over the European latecomers. In Russia, by the turn of the nineteenth century, the line of czars who ruled the area had wavered back and forth between tolerance and banishment in their laws regarding Jewish residents. One czar would banish Jews, the next would try to encourage them to settle in a specified area, and then the next tried to assimilate them.

The Jacob A. Riis Collection/Museum of the City of New York

This 1888 scene of Baxter Street on New York's Lower East Side is one of many photos Jacob A. Riis shot of the conditions urban tenement dwellers had to endure.

In the 1880s, most Russian Jews (which also included other eastern European Jews, because at this time, Russia ruled Poland and Romania) were living isolated lives in Jewish enclaves called shtetls. Many Russians were glad to keep the Jews inside the "Pale of Settlement" and rural environs outside the mainstream of Russian society. It is also true that the Orthodox rabbis who ruled these areas generally were also content to keep the Jews in their own separate society, under their control, outside the influence of modern (Western) ideas. The Orthodox rabbis feared losing their Jewish citizens to nineteenth-century influences. As a result, the ghetto walls kept the Jews inside and kept out modern times.

Of course the isolation was not complete. Some Jews had in fact abandoned the traditional Jewish way of life, but the vast majority had not.

With the ascension to power of Czar Alexander III in 1881, everything changed. His father, Alexander II, had been killed by terrorists, and the new czar blamed his father's death on Jewish dissidents. With the help of the procurator of the holy synod of the Orthodox Church—the infamous Konstantin Pobedonostsev—Alexander III drew up a long-range plan designed to totally eliminate Russian Jewry. One third of the Jews would be shipped overseas. One third would be converted to Christianity. The third that remained would be starved to death.

Pobedonostsev also institutionalized the pogrom—organized attacks by Russian cossacks on Jewish villages. Jews were killed in the streets and terrorized. As the violent pogroms increased in frequency and violence, Jewish life in Russia became a constant terror.

The Jews who abandoned Russia for passage to America didn't stream over in dribs and drabs—they came by the thousands. Entire villages packed up and boarded boats headed across the Atlantic. Historians differ on the exact numbers that immigrated; some say the average was at least fifty thousand a year for the forty years between 1881 and 1921. By the 1920s, North America was home to around two and a half million Russian Jews, more than ten times the number of resident German Jews.

The trip across the ocean was not easy for these refugees from Eastern Europe. Many—probably most—had never been more than a few miles away from home before. The crowded conditions on the boats were "almost unendurable." To save money on provisions, some unscrupulous boat owners even served them ham during the trip, knowing that because it wasn't kosher, it wouldn't be eaten.

The North American German Jews were as shocked at the wave of ragged newcomers as the newcomers were disoriented in their new surroundings. Many North American Jews reacted in horror as boat after boat disgorged what looked to them like ghosts from the Middle Ages—Jews with earlocks, yarmulkes, and Hasidic garb who spoke Yiddish and barely understood English. If these new arrivals weren't ghosts, they were certainly an unfamiliar sight to the German Jewish scions of North American society. These impoverished "masses yearning to breathe free" were an unexpected reminder of the Jewish past in Europe.

Russian Jews Crowd into the Lower East Side

Most of the boats carrying Russian Jewish immigrants across the Atlantic docked in New York harbor. Here, at Ellis Island, the majority of the Jewish passengers disembarked and headed for homes on Manhattan's Lower East Side. Of course, many entered the continent through other towns on the North American Atlantic coast—including Philadelphia, Boston, and Baltimore—but it is estimated that fully three-quarters of the flood of Russian Jews disembarked at New York City and lived, at least for a while, in the swarming slums of lower Manhattan.

Ellis Island had been constructed because of the arrival of this large mass of immigrants in the early 1890s. Originally, those who arrived had been processed at another location in New York harbor—Castle Garden—but as the numbers of people getting off the boats from Europe increased exponentially each year, Castle Garden, which had originally been built as a fort and had occasionally been used as a concert hall, proved too small to handle these substantial numbers of people. Even the expanded Ellis Island facilities, designated by the U.S. federal government as a national immigration center, turned out to be cramped quarters for the thousands of people that were soon treading its halls.

In the early 1900s, merchants selling from pushcarts were a common sight on the urban landscape, as seen in these views of Hester Street on New York's Lower East Side in 1894.

American Jewish Archives

American Jewish Archives

When Russian Jewish immigration to the U.S. was at its height, the Ellis Island reception hall was oftentimes overflowing.

The Ellis Island immigration center, which was restored and established as a museum in the late 1980s, is a cluster of ornate buildings. For many of the Jewish immigrants, arrival at this island was almost like landing on another planet. Impatient men in uniforms barked at them in English—a strange language that few of them knew. When their names were inscribed in the official record books, the disinterested officials often got the spellings hopelessly tangled, transforming foreign surnames into nearly unrecognizable English transliterations. Doctors examined the bewildered immigrants without explaining what they were looking for. Other brusque examiners demanded to know their political leanings and whether or not they had criminal backgrounds or more than one spouse.

The "wrong" answer to the hastily shouted questions or a questionable finding by one of the doctors could mean a return trip to Europe. Of course, most immigrants passed the tests. But some of those who failed and were to be sent back to the Old World killed themselves rather than set foot in Europe once again.

Near Ellis Island was another island that was to assume mythic proportions among the masses being processed for acceptance to the New World—Bedloe's Island, home of the Statue of Liberty. This lady with the upraised torch, a gift from the French, was dedicated in 1886, just in time to light the way for most of the new arrivals.

The famous poem inscribed on the base of the statue was written by a Sephardic New York Jew—Emma Lazarus. Originally a poetess who specialized in verse extolling traditional Greek ideals of beauty and truth, Lazarus had been shocked by graphic newspaper reports of Russian pogroms against Jews. Her poem "The New Colossus," a sonnet written during a fund-raising drive for the Statue of Liberty's pedestal, reflects the shift of her poetic focus as well as her feminism:

> Not like the brazen giant of Greek fame,
> With conquering limbs astride from land to land,
> Here at our sea-washed, sunset gates shall stand
> A mighty woman . . . .

It actually was not until 1903 that the sonnet, which was carved into a brass plaque, was fastened to the statue's base. Lazarus, who earned $1,500 for her fourteen-line poem, went on to become a dedicated Zionist as well as a Hebrew translator.

The Lower East Side—Teeming Ghetto

Why did the Russian Jews flock to the Lower East Side of Manhattan? The new settlement there was part historical accident and part convenience. The East Side's tenements were in close proximity to where most of the immigrants arrived, plenty of living space (albeit crowded) was available, and the housing was cheap enough for the impoverished immigrants to afford.

Although this East Side neighborhood had been a respectable place to live at the beginning of the 1800s, by the time of the Civil War it already had become the slum area for New York City's underclass. It was the acknowledged "ghetto," reserved for new arrivals who had no money. Before the waves of Russian Jews arrived, it had been mainly the home of Hungarian and gentile German expatriots. But by the time the nineteenth century ended and many Russian Jews had poured in, this part of town had become the most densely populated neighborhood in New York.

New York Public Library

© Evan Agostini

Although Emma Lazarus (top) wrote early poems celebrating classical themes, her later poems, such as "The New Colossus" (bottom), which is carved in a brass plaque on the Statue of Liberty, focus on the concerns of modern society.

American Jewish Archives

As life became increasingly intolerable for Jews living in Russia, more and more made the long trek to North America.

Census studies show that the Lower East Side's population density had already climbed to about 520 people per acre in the early 1890s. But by the turn of the century, that figure had climbed amazingly to over seven hundred. There were more than 330,000 people crammed into less than one square mile of city streets. Jacob Riis, a writer and activist who worked to improve conditions in the tenements, claimed that "nowhere in the world are so many people crowded together on a square mile as here." Like a giant human magnet, the community kept attracting more and more Jewish newcomers. People were packed into apartments like sardines.

Life in this crowded New World was strange and almost incomprehensible to the newcomers just off the boat from rural Russia. As one immigrant recalled, "I felt bewilderingly alien, for no two worlds could have been more stupendously unlike than the mud-sodden village from which I had been uprooted and the towering New York into which I was flung…the tall buildings…gas and electric lights that banished night…the horsecars and trolleys…the newsstands which sold enormous sized dailies at a penny each—an unbelievably low price for so much paper…"

For these teeming Jewish masses, the three main occupations were selling from a pushcart, sewing clothes in a garment factory, and peddling goods door-to-door.

The pushcarts filled the streets and made the sidewalks a noisy open-air bazaar. One newspaper reporter guessed that just on Orchard Street—one of the byways in the heart of the Jewish section—there were more than fifteen hundred pushcarts. You could buy almost anything you wanted off one of these carts: food, clothing, books, pins, scissors. None of the prices were fixed. Every transaction was a feisty negotiation. The seller quoted a high price for his wares. In response, the prospective buyer bid low. Together, after much haggling, the two came to an "understanding." Multiply that kind of energetic conversation by the hundreds, and you get a small idea of the hubbub of these neighborhoods.

Peddling was a more strenuous occupation. Peddlers reassured each other that the largest American retail millionaires had started this way—after all, hadn't the Guggenheims once sold wares to housewives? But after thousands of hopeful salesmen invaded New York apartment houses and then took to other parts of the country with silverware, pots and pans, and other household goods hanging from their backs, peddling became a tough way to earn a dollar. Some besieged housewives wouldn't answer the door if they thought a peddler was there.

One New York peddler said that to make a living he had to climb about two hundred flights of steps every day—and he must have gone down those steps, too. For his trouble, he made two dollars a day. That comes to about a penny per flight of steps. It was backbreaking work.

Tailoring and working in clothing factories were the most widespread Jewish occupations. As early as the 1890s, Jacob Riis claimed that "the Jewish needle made America the best-dressed nation in the world." Although few of these immigrants had worked full time at tailoring in Europe, many of them had worked at

The Jacob A. Riis Collection/Museum of the City of New York

This Jacob Riis photograph illustrates a typical day in the life of Lower East Siders—the immigrants were overcrowded and overworked.

least a little bit with needle and thread before crossing the Atlantic. Consequently, sewing was one trade they didn't need much training for. And in the United States, there seemed to be a never-ending need for workers who would bend over sewing machines all day.

The downtown garment shops—many of them owned by German Jews—were also convenient to the Lower East Side. Added to that, the new immigrants didn't have to speak English to get a job in one of the many "sweatshops" that seemed to be everywhere in the ghetto.

And the sweatshops lived up to their names. The work never ceased, and the conditions were as cramped, hot, and dirty as the tenements the workers called home. In a short story written by one of the immigrants, he claimed, "The day isn't twenty-four hours long, it's twelve coats."

Riis said that if you rode through the Lower East Side on the elevated train along Second Avenue, you traveled by a half mile of clothing factories. "Every open window of the big tenements, that stand like a continuous brick wall on both sides of the way, give you a glimpse of men and women bending over their [sewing] machines or ironing clothes at the window, half-naked."

Factory owners crammed workers into every space available. Sometimes workers even toiled on the roof. The bosses worked their employees day and night, seven days a week—though sometimes they let them have Saturday off. Both the employees and the contractors who stood over them were hungry for a piece of the American dream. To get your piece, you had to have money. To have money, you had to work and work and work. And then work some more.

Sixty- to eighty-hour workweeks were common. Plus, workers would take sewing home and piece together more garments—sometimes until the wee hours of the morning. The situation was definitely exploitive, the working conditions horrendous. But the bosses were Jews—they spoke the same language as the workers—and many of the immigrants didn't know what other kinds of jobs they could get because they couldn't communicate well in English.

Making matters worse, the constant flood of new immigrants not only kept wages from increasing but drove them down. In the first part of the 1880s, a semi-skilled garment worker could pull in about fifteen dollars a week. By the middle of the decade, workers were averaging about half that, although a very good worker might get ten dollars a week. In any case, women made only 50 percent of the meager wage that men earned. Fortunately, the pay gradually rose again as the American market for ready-to-wear clothes increased, but it was still a hard way to earn money.

This tumultuous urban collection of sewing factories helped break down the old social order. As one writer pointed out, "They succeeded who put aside the old preconceptions, pushed in and took care of themselves." A wild, free-form capitalism was unleashed upon a population who worked hard but who also gave careful thought to the meaning of their changed lives.

The Byron Collection/Museum of the City of New York

In a short story about mythical Jewish immigrants from a town called Kuzmin, Sholem Asch, one of the most famous Jewish writers of the time, described how the sweatshop ruthlessly eliminated old social distinctions and introduced new ones: "[What had been] the whole village of Kuzmin worked upstairs in Uncle Moses' shop.... All Kuzmin sat there sewing for Uncle Moses; he had reduced the entire population to the same level. There were no more leading citizens, synagogue dignitaries, and humble artisans—no more Talmudic experts and coarse fellows.... All now served a single idol; all performed the same rite—they sewed trousers."

The rapid rate of social change was probably enhanced by the fact that everyone lived on top of each other. Life in the garment factory as well as in the tenement was inescapably crowded. A survey of families in the early 1900s showed that 25 percent of the Lower East Side residents slept two to a room while half of the families crammed three or four into a bedroom. The other 25 percent had five or more people bedding down in each room every night. To save money, any family who had an apartment brought in boarders who shared the rent.

This tight conglomeration of people made for a noisy, dirty, and malodorous as well as stimulating and exciting urban environment. Yet, even though disease was a serious public health problem throughout the city and tuberculosis was referred to as the "tailor's disease," the statistics of the time seem to indicate that the Jewish population had fewer health problems than the other urban ethnic groups.

For instance, figures compiled in the early 1900s show that Russian Jews suffered only about half of the tuberculosis-related deaths as other New Yorkers did. The reason for this healthiness is a mystery. Some historians attribute Jewish hardiness to their deprived lives in the European ghettos—these people were already used to withstanding harsh conditions. Others claim that the Jewish customs of self-denial became health habits that helped them survive. Jews rarely imbibed alcohol except on ceremonial occasions. The Jewish kosher laws—which prohibited ham and shellfish—made them very particular about what they ate.

Another possible explanation is that the support Jews received from their relatives aided their health. The family unit was revered and seldom broken up in separation or divorce. Perhaps the psychological reinforcement they received from their sturdy family structures helped them pull through this tough time.

Other historians explain the Jewish hardiness by pointing to their belief in progress: Russian Jews had been dirt-poor in Eastern Europe. In the New World, they were crowded and poorly paid, but they didn't have to fear the pogrom. There surely was anti-Semitism in North America, but they didn't have to fear government-sponsored anti-Semitic attacks. They weren't making much money, but they were saving some for a better future. Today's work was hard, but their children would enjoy a better life. This hope for tomorrow may have been the medicine that kept their death rate down. They believed that they had something to live for.

New York's Hester Street epitomized life on the Lower East Side.

66

CHAPTER SIX

The Jewish Labor Movement

Out of the sweatshops of the Lower East Side emerged some Jewish newcomers who made a fortune in the clothing business. But an even more significant development than the accumulated wealth of these individuals was the mass labor movement that evolved in this neighborhood. In retrospect, it may seem that the Jewish union movement was an inevitable result of the exploitive labor practices prevalent in the sweatshops. But in fact, initial efforts at unionizing these workers seemed doomed.

At the turn of the century, the labor leaders who tried to organize unions among the workers on the Lower East Side had a difficult time. Every time the garment market improved, wages would climb temporarily and workers would forsake the union. When wages dropped, workers joined but showed no real long-term interest in being unionized.

The International Ladies Garment Workers Union (ILGWU), which was to be one of the most important of these organizations, was started in 1900 at a meeting of only eleven delegates. For the next ten years, this union and others were barely able to keep going. Members were hard to find and harder to keep.

Similarly, during the first decade of the twentieth century, the United Hebrew Trades (UHT), the central organization of Jewish unions, barely had five thousand scattered members. And despite the fact that Samuel Gompers, a Jew born in England, was a powerful force in the more well-established American Federation of Labor (AFL), the nascent UHT initially got very little help from these other union organizations.

Gompers had come to the United States in 1863 with his family. He had entered the work force at age ten, in London, as a shoemaker. At sixteen, he began work in a cigar-making factory in New York City. By the 1870s, he was deeply involved with the cigar-makers' union. As president of his local, he led a successful strike for better working conditions in 1877.

Samuel Gompers was an important leader of the American Federation of Labor.

American Jewish Archives

In 1886, Gompers was instrumental in forming the national organization of workers called the American Federation of Labor. This conglomeration of trade and labor unions fought and won the struggle for eight-hour workdays, better wages, and safer working conditions for its members.

The conservative Gompers and his colleagues were not entirely comfortable with the new Jewish immigrants who formed the UHT. They distrusted the UHT's leftist, socialist leanings. And while the UHT fought for unrestricted immigration laws, the AFL was opposed to letting so many immigrants into the country, afraid it would take away jobs from the workers already living in the United States.

Although Gompers did offer his support to the garment workers in New York City, the UHT and its member unions were generally isolated from the mainstream American labor movement because of their philosophical and social conflicts. As the 1900s began, they were on their own, limping along with few members, seemingly never to become a powerful force on the American labor scene.

During the first part of the twentieth century, many Jewish immigrants found employment in crowded sweatshops, where they were paid meager wages for long hours. These small factories were not restricted to New York's Lower East Side. This shop, owned by Abraham Krevetz, was on Lloyd Street in Baltimore.

AP/Wide World Photos

International Ladies Garment Workers' Union Archives, Labor-Management Documentation Center, Cornell University

In 1909, the Jewish labor movement gathered unprecedented force and momentum. This rally at Union Square in New York City was one of the first giant demonstrations signifying the movement's immense support among workers.

Then, toward the end of 1909, the attitude among Jewish workers changed. Rather than resisting the labor organizations, they suddenly welcomed and even demanded unions. Historians are largely at a loss, however, to explain exactly why this change occurred. In 1909, times were good. Garment sales were up. Some historians feel that these improved conditions actually gave the workers the security they needed to strike. With a few dollars in the bank, perhaps workers thought they could withstand wageless periods during a strike.

Another explanation may be found in the changing nature of the workplace. During this time, the number of small sweatshops in the tenements had declined. Their replacements—larger, but still crowded, loft factories—were just as uncomfortable as the loosely organized tenement apartment workshops they replaced, but the atmosphere was more impersonal.

It is possible that these new, bigger establishments gave birth to a more remote management system that encouraged workers to band together in self-defense. In the smaller sweatshops, workers had been on a first-name basis with their bosses. Conditions had been bad, but workers felt they had something in common with their bosses, who worked alongside them. Once the factories grew, it became harder to identify with supervisors. They were now bureaucrats who gave orders to a crowd of employees. Fewer workers knew their bosses personally. In that new, colder atmosphere, joining the union probably seemed a more reasonable way for workers to stand up for themselves.

Once the labor movement started expanding, it heated up like a nuclear reaction—the increasing numbers of unionized workers and their frustrations growing to the point where they fomented a social chain reaction.

Uprising of the Twenty Thousand

In a famous meeting at Cooper Union in New York City on November 22, 1909, one group of workers actually took the lead away from their labor leaders. To the surprise of the more restrained union officials, they called for a strike. This spontaneous uprising came from a most unexpected source: young, female blouse-makers.

At that time, blouses were called shirtwaists. The women who made shirtwaists were usually in their teens or early twenties. The general consensus among labor leaders and factory owners was that these young women couldn't be successfully organized into effective unions because they were too young. They were only interested in finding a good husband, said the proverbial wisdom. As usual, the proverbial wisdom was wrong.

In the early years of the twentieth century, the shirtwaist business had grown substantially. Because of the changing taste in fashions, the number of factories making shirtwaists multiplied. A marginal business in 1900, shirtwaist sales topped $50 million by the time of the Cooper Union meeting.

In 1909, due to this recent expansion of the shirtwaist business, working conditions for the shirtwaist "girls" were actually better than they were for many other garment workers. The factories they worked in were practically new. The lofts were wired for electricity, while many of the older shops still relied on the workers' feet to run the treadle-powered sewing machines.

Still, the women in the shirtwaist factories had many legitimate complaints. Out of their measly few dollars a week, they had to pay for their own needles and supplies. They paid "rent" for the chairs they sat on and the lockers where they hung their clothes. They paid fines if they were a few minutes late for work. They even had to pay for the electricity they used to make the shirtwaists!

Before calling the general meeting of shirtwaist-makers at Cooper Union, the ILGWU Local 25, which consisted of women in the industry, had already staged some limited job actions against individual employers. These actions had not accomplished anything meaningful. In each case, the factory owners had intimidated their workers with scabs and thugs.

The meeting at Cooper Union was a general meeting of all the shirtwaist workers, not merely members of Local 25 (which had only about a hundred members at the time). It was standing room only, but the crowd was disappointed. The speakers were uninspiring. As the meeting proceeded, the union leadership droned on and on in a procession of platitudinous speeches that offered little vision and no concrete plan of action.

Finally, a teenager in the audience, Clara Lemlich, a worker who was involved in a long, frustrating strike against a factory owned by the Lierson family (she had been beaten while on the picket line), stood up and began her own passionate call for a general strike against all the shirtwaist companies.

In Yiddish, she implored the crowd to stop being so passive: "I am a working girl, striking against intolerable conditions. I am tired of listening to speakers who spout generalities. We are here to decide to strike or not to strike. I resolve that a general strike be declared—now!"

The crowd responded enthusiastically, waving handkerchiefs, stamping its feet, jumping up and down. Benjamin Feigenbaum, chairman of the meeting, called for order but was drowned out. When he finally asked if there were any seconds, the uproar in the hall started anew, the entire crowd screaming assent.

Swept on this tide of passion, Feigenbaum asked the crowd to swear its loyalty. "Do you mean this in good faith?" he asked. "Will you take the old Jewish pledge?" The crowd was a sea of raised hands as everyone swore with him: "If I turn traitor to the cause I now pledge, may my right hand wither from this arm I now raise."

This strike became known as the Uprising of the Twenty Thousand. Women walked out of more than five hundred shops and joined picket lines. Jewish socialists and feminists rallied to the cause. Members of the Women's Trade Union League, a feminist and labor organization funded by middle-class women, joined the Jewish and Italian workers on the picket line.

To the surprise of many Americans, women were active in the labor unions. Here, female workers march on the Lower East Side.

Rallies were held all over New York City during the 1909 shirtwaist workers' strike.

The shop owners called the police. In those years, the police regularly intimidated strikers and broke up job actions. More than seven hundred workers were arrested. During the strike, the union spent more than $2,000 a day bailing out its members. But the strike received international attention. A judge sent workers to jail, saying, "You are on strike against God and Nature, whose firm law is that man shall earn his bread in the sweat of his brow." Responding to this news by telegram, George Bernard Shaw said, "Delightful. Medieval America always in the intimate personal confidence of the Almighty."

The factory owners didn't rely entirely on the police—they also hired thugs to intimidate the picketers. In a common scenario, the goons would attack the picketers, fighting would break out, the cops would arrive and arrest only the picketers for fighting. During the melee, strike breakers would enter the factory.

The strike spread to Philadelphia. Funds for the union were raised across the country. Women at Wellesley contributed a thousand dollars. The dedicated union women addressed groups everywhere, evoking praise and respect for "our wonderful girls."

Despite the fervent emotions raised by the strike, it petered out in February 1910. During the strike, some of the smaller firms had negotiated settlements early on. The larger factories conceded some points, but did not actually come around to officially recognizing the union as a collective bargaining agent for the workers.

But the union had solid gains it could point to—working conditions had improved. Union membership in ILGWU Local 25 had climbed a hundredfold to ten thousand. And passionate life had been breathed into the Jewish labor movement. There was a new sense of togetherness among workers. There was a new perception of what workers, united, could accomplish against employers who had once appeared invincible.

Protocol of Peace

It was only a matter of time before the next labor action. What the shirtwaist women had done spontaneously, the cloak-makers set about carefully planning.

Cloak-making in 1910 was predominantly a male profession. It was also a much larger and more prominent industry than shirtwaist manufacturing. There were sixty thousand cloak-makers in New York, three times as many as the workers who produced shirtwaists.

Soon after the shirtwaist strike ended, the cloak-makers began to save up a strike fund. While the shirtwaist women had met at Cooper Union, the cloak-makers gathered at Madison Square Garden—and not everyone could fit in. Thousands had to stand outside as the meeting progressed.

By the time the strike was called in the beginning of July 1910, the cloak-makers had about $250,000 in their strike fund. The chief fund-raiser was Morris Winchevsky, a Yiddish poet. (As Irving Howe, who has written widely about Jewish history of the nineteenth and twentieth centuries, pointed out: "Where but in the Yiddish world could a poet have been chief fund-raiser for a general strike?")

On July 7, 1910, the cloak-makers walked off the job. Abraham Rosenberg, president of ILGWU, said the first few minutes of the strike, which began at 2 P.M., were awe-inspiring moments: "We saw a sea of people surging out of the side streets toward Fifth Avenue.... In my mind I could only picture to myself such a scene taking place when the Jews were led out of Egypt."

The union demanded better working conditions, higher wages, and a shorter workweek. But the real sticking point was the demand for a closed shop. The strikers wanted employers only to hire union members. While the other demands seemed amenable to negotiation, the employers refused to budge on the issue of only hiring union workers.

As July turned into August and the strike continued, it looked like the strikers and the owners would both strangle in debt and bankruptcy. The strike fund dwindled. Factory owners were unable to meet contracts.

At the end of the summer, both sides decided to have their grievances settled by arbitration. A committee headed by Louis Brandeis, a prominent Jewish lawyer from Boston and future Supreme Court justice, worked out a compromise agreement. Instead of a closed shop, both sides settled for a "preferential shop." Union standards for working conditions would be required in the factories and union members would be preferentially hired over nonunion workers. This famous agreement was called the "Protocol of Peace." It was signed on Friday, September 2, 1910.

That Friday, the agreement inspired an all-night party on the streets of the Lower East Side. Crowds sang, hugged each other, and congratulated one and all until dawn. Then the party started again on Saturday afternoon. The tenement dwellers had graduated from exploited sweatshop employees to a disciplined, organized force to be reckoned with.

A succession of strikes followed as other industries organized themselves. The spirit of the Jewish labor movement soared. And then horrible tragedy crushed it in grief.

In many instances, women played a leading role in much of the early union activity among New York's Jewish workers.

The Flames of the New Inquisition

The Triangle Shirtwaist Company was one of the biggest garment factories in New York City. Probably the largest shirtwaist manufacturer, this firm employed more than eight hundred workers, mostly women, on three upper floors of a loft building on Greene Street and Washington Place, in the southeast corner of Greenwich Village.

On March 25, 1911, about an hour before quitting time, a careless smoker at the Triangle Company dropped a match that set fire to fabric scraps on the floor. When workers tried to fight the fire with an emergency fire hose, it fell apart in their hands. The fire quickly reached the volatile cleaning fluids stored in the factory. They were set aflame and the inferno reached unbearable temperatures.

Some workers tried to pound their way out through the exits in the rear, but they were locked. The owners of the factory restricted entrance and exit to the shop. Before anyone went home, they had to be searched to make sure they weren't stealing.

At a meeting at New York City's Cooper Union in 1909, the women who made shirtwaists (blouses) shocked the labor world by calling for a general strike.

American Jewish Archives

The fire escape available to Triangle workers was a single, narrow ladder that led up to the roof. Despite the smoke and fire and confusion, about seventy of the women succeeded in navigating this route to the roof and safety. Some escaped on the elevator. The elevator operator ferried as many as he could to lower floors before the fire destroyed the cables.

Even though the fire department arrived on the scene about ten minutes after the alarm had been given, there was little they could do to save workers trapped in the building. Their ladders didn't reach the floors on fire—and neither did the water from their hoses.

The disaster was a heartbreaking scene of death and despair. Firemen spread their nets to catch the women jumping from the flames, but the momentum of the falling bodies was too great and they plunged through the nets to the sidewalk.

A reporter at the scene told of how a man at a window helped the women jump from the inferno: "They were all as unresisting as if he were helping them into a street car instead of into eternity.... He brought another girl to the window. I saw her put her arms around him and kiss him. Then he held her out into space—and dropped her. Quick as a flash, he was on the windowsill himself. His coat fluttered upward—the air filled his trouser legs as he came down. I could see he wore tan shoes…his hat remained on his head."

Some resisted jumping to certain death and only yielded to the long drop when the conflagration engulfed them. The same reporter said, "These torches, suffering ones, fell inertly, only intent that death should come to them on the sidewalk instead of in the furnace behind them. The floods of water from the firemen's hose that ran into the gutter were actually stained red with blood."

In the end, 146 died; they were mostly young Jewish and Italian women. Some were burned beyond recognition. The owners of the factory were tried for manslaughter but acquitted.

Rose Schneiderman, an eloquent member of the Women's Trade Union, compared factories like Triangle to the Spanish Inquisition the Jews had fled in the 1600s when they first came to North America: "The old Inquisition had its rack and its thumbscrews and its instruments of torture with iron teeth. We know what these things are today: the iron teeth are our necessities, the thumbscrews are the high-powered and swift machinery close to which we must work, and the rack is here in the firetrap structures that will destroy us the minute they catch fire…."

But the terrible tragedy had beneficial consequences. New York City conducted a full-scale investigation of factory conditions and soon revamped its fire code and its requirements for building construction (the building that housed the Triangle Shirtwaist Company had supposedly been fireproof). City factory inspections were tightened. Requirements for employer liability insurance were expanded and workmen's compensation rules were enhanced.

And the Jewish unions gathered more energy. The conflagration spurred the labor movement on to new heights and power.

American Jewish Archives

In 1911, a fire at the Triangle Shirtwaist Company in New York City killed 146 workers—most of them young women who jumped to their deaths. Exit doors that could have saved lives had been locked.

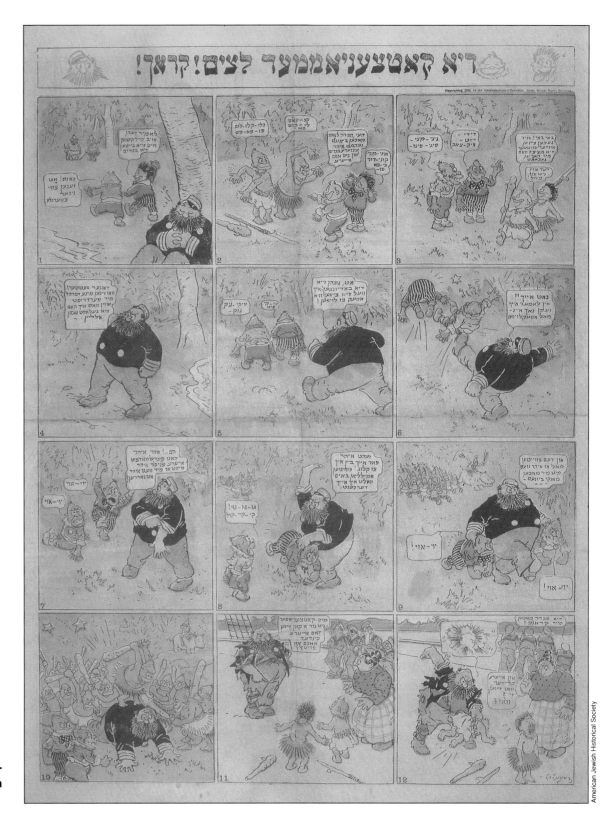

Translated from English into Yiddish, the "Katzenjammer Clowns Crash" and their adventures in Africa appeared in the *Jewish American* in 1906.

CHAPTER SEVEN.

Jewish-American Journalism

Early North American Jewish Journalism

At the turn of the century, the teeming masses of recent Jewish immigrants to North America represented more than merely the large-scale transplantation of people from one part of the world to another. Out of its sheer size and interaction of new ideas and life-styles, this huge new settlement gave birth to a community whose creativity influenced the world's cultural development. And from the roiling sprawl of Jewish immigrants living in the Lower East Side of Manhattan—and the adjacent Jewish settlement in Brooklyn—innovations in journalism, literature, entertainment, and even crime emerged that would have powerful long-range effects on North America.

In the field of journalism, one Jewish daily newspaper was fated to stand out as dominant in the history of Russian Jewish immigration: the *Jewish Daily Forward,* which was started in 1897.

Before the appearance of the *Forward,* there had been many periodicals expressing various Jewish points of view, but none became as popular or enjoyed such long-lasting influence as the *Forward* was destined to have.

Part of the reason that few publications aimed at a Jewish audience did not survive for long was that prior to the 1880s, the North American Jewish population was rather small and hard-pressed to support many periodicals. For instance, for two years, from 1824 to 1826, S. H. Jackson had published a periodical called *The Jew,* whose purpose was to counter efforts by some Christian organizations to convert Jews to Christianity. Because of its limited aims and audience, this publication soon went out of business.

Library of Congress

Isaac Leeser, whom some consider to be the real founding father of Jewish journalism in the New World, found more sustained success with a monthly publication called *The Occident,* which he started in 1843.

Leeser was born in Westphalia, Germany, in 1806. At the age of eighteen, he emigrated to Richmond, Virginia, where he found a job as an accountant. By the 1830s, however, he was writing articles about anti-Semitism. These writings and his rising enthusiasm for espousing new ideas about American Judaism far surpassed his interest in accounting. Eventually he secured a job as the cantor at the Mikveh Israel synagogue in Philadelphia.

From his post in Philadelphia, Leeser established himself as a progressive Jewish activist. While he continued to believe that Jews should pray in Hebrew, he translated the Hebrew prayers so that congregants, most of whom did not understand a word of Hebrew, could know what they were saying at services. He also gave his sermons in English instead of the conventional German.

Besides publishing *The Occident,* Leeser tried to start a Hebrew day school, a Jewish publication society, and a Hebrew college. All of these endeavors quickly folded, but *The Occident* had a broad impact on Jews across the continent and stimulated much debate over how Judaism could adapt to modern times. In the pages of *The Occident,* Leeser advocated changes in Orthodox practices but was not as radical in his positions as some in the Reform movement spearheaded by Isaac Wise. He tried to be a Jewish compromiser and hoped that the Orthodox and Reform wings of American Judaism would join together in a mutually acceptable coalition.

Of course, Reform and Orthodox never did fuse and this dream of Leeser's was never realized, but he could count among his accomplishments a highly successful English translation of the Torah. Up until the 1900s, his translation was the most widespread English version of the Torah read by American Jews. Leeser also was appointed president of Maimonides College, a school he helped found.

The Occident came out every month from 1843 until 1868. Although historians fault it for an uninteresting style, its continent-wide circulation helped promote a feeling of Jewish unity in North America.

While *The Occident* tried to find a middle ground between Reform and Orthodox stands on religious beliefs and practices, other eighteenth-century Jewish publications generally aligned themselves with one or the other of these two opposing sides or, in an effort to alienate no one, took no stand at all. *Israels Herold,* a weekly publication printed in German, was started in the spring of 1849 in New York. This periodical, headed by Isidor Busch, a New York abolitionist, tried to promote the unity of American Jews by taking Reform positions. Busch chronicled the occupations of American Jews and pushed for more aid to new immigrants, but the weekly only lasted for about twelve issues.

Soon after *Israels Herold* closed in the fall of 1849, another Jewish weekly out of New York, the *Asmonean,* began publication. This paper was in English and was

THE OCCIDENT,

AND

AMERICAN JEWISH ADVOCATE.

A MONTHLY PERIODICAL

DEVOTED TO

THE DIFFUSION OF KNOWLEDGE

ON

Jewish Literature and Religion.

EDITED

BY ISAAC LEESER.

ללמוד וללמד לשמור ולעשות
"To learn and to teach, to observe and to do."

VOL. I.

PHILADELPHIA:
PUBLISHED AT 118 SOUTH FOURTH STREET.
5604.

American Jewish Archives

Isaac Leeser (opposite) was a progressive Jewish activist who founded the monthly publication *The Occident.*

Sinai.

Ein Organ

für

Erkenntniß und Veredlung des Judenthums,

in monatlichen Heften

herausgegeben von

Dr. David Einhorn,

Rabbiner der Har-Sinai-Gemeinde zu Baltimore.

את אחי אנכי מבקש

Meine Brüder suche ich. — Genes. 37, 16.

Pränumerationspreis für das ganze Jahr $2,00.

Zweiter Jahrgang.

Baltimore.

Gedruckt bei C. W. Schneidereith No. 22 Sharp-Straße.
1858.

edited by Robert Lyon, who had been born in England. Lyon decided to remain editorially neutral in the struggle between Reform and Orthodox believers. Lyon gave space on the pages of his periodical to both sides of the Reform-Orthodox conflict and allowed his writers to present opposing viewpoints. This journalistic formula—printing in English and giving both sides of the issue—made the weekly a national success. It was soon accepted as the Jewish paper of record. For American Jews who wanted to be informed about the latest happenings in Jewish ideas and culture, it was a must-read.

The *Asmonean* stayed in business for nine years until a plethora of competing publications took away most of its readership and put it out of business. From Cincinnati, Isaac Wise, who headed the Reform movement, published both the *American Israelite* and *Die Deborah*, a German publication. From Baltimore, a periodical called the *Sinai*, which also advocated Reform Judaism, was started. At the same time, in New York, an Orthodox publication, *The Jewish Messenger*, was successful in gaining wide readership.

The Jewish Messenger started an important trend in Jewish journalism because it published Jewish fiction and poetry, not just current events and religious stands. It also took positions on issues that affected social welfare by pushing for the establishment of orphanages, improving certain New York charities, and setting up a Jewish Free School.

Besides these national journals, publications catering to local Jewish interests also began to proliferate in the mid-nineteenth century. This carried over to the West Coast, and by 1860, San Francisco was home to two Jewish newspapers, the *Voice of Israel*—started in 1856—and the *Weekly Gleaner*, which was begun in 1857.

Yiddish Journalism

The large influx of Russian Jews in the late 1800s gave rise to Jewish newspapers printed in Yiddish. As a language, Yiddish is generally a mixture of German, English, Hebrew, and a smattering of all the other Romance languages. According to Irving Howe, the prominent chronicler of Jewish history, the creation of Yiddish flowed near and beneath Hebrew, which had traditionally been the Jews' sacred language and the language of prayers and the Torah: "Elbowed away from the place of honor, it [Yiddish] grew freely and richly, based originally on a mixture of Middle High German dialects...."

Yiddish had been the language of the Jewish settlements and ghettos in Russia and Eastern Europe. As soon as the language was imported into North America, it changed again, adopting many American-English phrases. In the 1870s, Yiddish papers that used a type of Yiddish almost identical to that spoken in Europe began to appear in New York and other cities. By the turn of the century, there were nearly a hundred Yiddish newspapers in North America.

American Jewish Archives

The first substantial Yiddish paper was probably *Die Yidishe Gazeten,* a weekly begun by Kasriel Sarasohn in 1874. It was designed for readers who wanted to preserve their connection to Europe. Sold in delicatessens, groceries, and butcher shops, it included a calendar of community and synagogue events and carried essays about religious feelings. Its Yiddish was "upper-class" Yiddish, with few slang expressions or colloquialisms.

Politicized, left-wing Yiddish publications were soon to follow. In 1890, the *Arbeiter-Zeitung,* a socialist weekly, and *Freie Arbeiter Stime,* an anarchist organ, were selling on the streets of New York. In order to appeal to the proletariat, these papers employed a "lower" form of Yiddish, closer to the version that was spoken in the neighborhoods where their readers lived.

Die Yidishe Gazeten gave birth to the *Yidishes Tageblat,* a daily paper, that employed the slogan "Preserve the purity of the Jewish family" as its rallying cry. Finding enemies of the Jewish people on every side, this paper found great success by 1895. It attacked socialists and anarchists as atheists who were trying to undermine the Jewish community. It warned its Jewish readership of the corruption and temptations of the gentile world.

John Paley, the colorful editor of *Yidishes Tageblat,* owned by Kasriel Sarasohn, found that he could sell more papers by embroidering the news with a sensationalist slant than by straight reporting. In one famous incident, Paley fed oysters to an unsuspecting, naive Jewish peddler as a prank. When told he had eaten nonkosher shellfish, the peddler became ill, threw up, and took to bed for several days. In *Yidishes Tageblat,* Paley reported the story as an attack on the man by anti-Semitic gangsters who had forced the oysters down the man's throat. When other journalists revealed the truth about the incident, Paley attacked those publications as atheistic rags out to undermine his reputation.

Paley's prolific, outrageous style made his paper the most popular of the Yiddish press at the time. Even though he frequently disappeared for several days at a time on alcoholic sprees, he was a publishing phenomenon who could crank out serialized novels, screaming editorials, and fanciful news items at an astonishing rate.

Beginning in 1897, the *Jewish Daily Forward* emerged from this pluralistic melting pot of Yiddish publications. Ostensibly, the *Forward* began its life as a socialist daily paper. But its founders, Abraham Cahan and Louis Miller, wanted the paper to avoid being controlled by political ax grinders. They wanted a paper responsive to the needs of Jewish immigrants who were trying to cope with long working days and the difficulties of adjusting to life in North America.

Very quickly, Cahan decided he should control the editorial direction of the *Forward.* Cahan, a strong-willed man, had been born near Vilna, in Russia, in 1860 and had been driven out by the anti-Semitic activities of the Russian czar Alexander III in 1882. He came to New York, learned English, and established himself as a writer. Some of his first pieces were printed in *Arbeiter-Zeitung,* a United Hebrew Trades publication.

Although Louis Miller (above) founded the *Jewish Daily Forward* with Abraham Cahan (opposite), Cahan soon eclipsed Miller as the paper's leading editor.

Cahan's editorial leadership of the *Forward* alienated many of his friends. While they saw the paper as an opportunity to air political grievances and take socialist positions on the issues of the day, Cahan was determined to walk more toward the middle of the political road (while leaning to the left). He was more interested in circulation gains than ideological hairsplitting. To do that, he made the paper into an introductory guide to American living for Eastern European Jews living on the Lower East Side.

Initially, Cahan's efforts at shaping the paper to his own vision failed. After less than a year, he resigned from the *Forward* and went to work for Lincoln Steffens as a reporter for the *Commercial Advertiser,* a job he held for five years. In this job, Cahan spent his time investigating different aspects of New York City life.

Without Cahan as editor, the *Forward* foundered. When he returned to the paper in 1902, he was given complete control over its editorial content. As its editor, his first job was to build circulation and take away the *Yidishes Tageblat*'s position as the leading Yiddish newspaper. The ensuing journalistic battle was fought at high volume.

The *Tageblat* took the position that the *Forward* was a dangerously radical paper that meant to abandon traditional Jewish morality for mean-spirited American commercial values. According to Paley, editor of the *Tageblat,* the *Forward* (and all its socialist fellow travelers) "wallowed" in radical life-styles that accepted free love and was out to "defile" Jewish family life.

Meanwhile, the *Forward* dug up dirt about Paley and his boss Sarasohn. It accused Sarasohn of using political connections to get a job for his brother from Tammany Hall (the New York political machine that had been built by "Boss" Tweed). It accused Paley of converting to Christianity in his youth.

Gradually, Cahan's publication prevailed, probably because his journalism espoused views more compatible to the left-wing, socialist-influenced perspective of the majority of Lower East Siders. And while the stories in the *Forward* tended to occasionally embellish the facts, the basic material was based on the real lives of his readers; the articles didn't rely on the unrestrained flights of fancy that Paley had used for so long.

Cahan's success brought criticism and envy from the Jewish intelligentsia who thought that while he was closer to their views than Paley had been, he pandered to the interests of the lowest common denominator. In their view, he was too concerned with keeping circulation up and paid too little attention to keeping intellectual standards high. Cahan's answer was that his more mundane features kept his readers' attention. And what good was a politically correct, intelligent newspaper if no one read it?

To the consternation of some of the more refined Jewish writers, the *Forward* also utilized a Yiddish that was close to what was spoken on the streets of New York. While Yiddish that stuck close to German was considered more cultured, Cahan liked to include "Englishisms" that had found their way into the language.

Cahan's genius was in focusing on his audience's needs rather than being interested in a political position. Many times, he co-opted his newspaper's competition by adopting and using to best advantage innovations they had thought up. For instance, in 1905, some of his own writers and editors—including Louis Miller, who had cofounded the *Forward*—had quit to start another daily paper, the *Warheit* (the "Truth"). In this paper, Miller printed letters from readers who sought advice for personal problems. From observing Miller's letters-to-the-editor column, Cahan got the idea for a column of his own, which he called the "Bintel Brief" (Bundle of Letters). The column was slow to gain in popularity, but when it finally won acceptance from readers, it became the most distinctive and widely read feature of the *Forward*. In the beginning, Cahan had his own writers invent some of the letters. But soon there was no need for invention—the mail was overwhelming.

The letters to this "Miss Lonelyhearts" type of column were mostly from Jewish women. They touched on every aspect of immigrant life—love, jobs, wives, husbands, fidelity, children, sex, health, morality, and religion. The column provided an incisive look at the issues and dilemmas that were on readers' minds. It was so popular, in fact, that it spawned a cottage industry of its own—writers hired themselves out to illiterate immigrants to write letters for them to the Bintel Brief.

In answer to the letters, the column offered practical advice, lessons in socialism, and tips on how to get by in New York. In its heyday, it was probably true that many readers picked up the *Forward* just to read the Bintel Brief.

While Cahan was building the *Forward* into the indisputable leading newspaper of the Lower East Side, other newspaper barons made futile attempts to grab some of the money and influence to be had in this market. William Randolph Hearst tried to start a paper called the *Yidisher Amerikaner*. While he made Jacob Pfeffer, a Jewish journalist, the editor-in-chief, the paper, whose journalism displayed little or no understanding of its audience, never got anywhere.

Another futile attempt at starting a downtown paper was made by New York German Jews. This paper, owned by wealthy "uptown" investors, including the Guggenheims and the Lehmans, was designed to civilize and gentrify the downtown Russian-Jewish crowd. In setting up the paper, these wealthy New Yorkers picked all the right men—the publication was headed by Louis Marshall, a man with long experience in various Jewish organizations, a tireless fighter for Jewish rights, and a staunch opponent of anti-Semitism. The editor was Zvi Hirsch Masliansky, another well-known activist.

But the operating principles of *Die Yidishe Velt* (Jewish World), as the paper was called, turned out to be a recipe for failure. Marshall said the paper would be "clean, wholesome [and] religious in tone"—in a word: boring. The publication's political position was conservative Republican, the least popular stance among the Lower East Siders. Even though the paper paid its editorial staff twenty-five dollars a week and up—the best wages of all the Yiddish publications—they were unable to both satisfy the "wholesome" requirements of the paper and still turn out interesting stories.

While *Die Yidishe Velt* was a decisive journalistic failure and lost large sums of money—at least $100,000 in its three years of existence—it did succeed in one thing: It managed to become the one issue that the *Forward* and the *Tageblat* agreed on. Both papers hated the *Velt* and vilified it. They both rejoiced when the *Velt* finally folded.

The Yiddish papers in the United States also inspired Yiddish publications in Canada. The *Kanader Yid* spread news of Jewish community affairs in Winnipeg. Similarly, the *Kanader Adler* was the Yiddish newspaper of Montreal, while the *Zhurnal* circulated in Toronto.

Foreign Affairs and the Yiddish Press

In the first part of the twentieth century, foreign affairs proved to be a tricky subject for the *Forward,* just as it was for many socialist Jews who had fled to North America to escape the persecution in Russia. At the beginning of World War I, the *Forward* and most of the other Yiddish papers were strongly pro-German. No Jew had a good word for the Russians who had driven them out. On the other hand, Germany was looked upon as a civilized center of culture.

The *Forward*'s opposition to U.S. entry into the war on the side of the Allies and Russia brought the paper into conflict with the American federal government. The government severely restricted the rights of dissenters and was imprisoning or deporting many of those who disagreed with its policies. In the conflict, the paper was threatened with losing the discounted mailing rights normally accorded to periodicals. To keep the right to distribute the *Forward* through the mail, Cahan agreed to abstain from attacking the government's position on the war and the draft. Cahan's retreat under government pressure inflamed many of the more radical socialists among its readers and contributors, but it kept the paper in business.

The *Forward*'s political position vis-à-vis the Russian Revolution also set the scene for editorial backtracking and second-guessing. Initially, Cahan was enthusiastic about Lenin and his communist takeover of Russia. Despite Lenin's brutality and repression, Cahan viewed communism as an improvement over the czars, who had governed the region for hundreds of years.

Cahan's support of the Bolsheviks stirred acrimonious debate among the Jewish community and on the editorial pages of the *Forward,* where both pro and con positions were printed. While Cahan admitted that the Russian communists were ruthless and had brutally murdered many of their opponents, his position, like many other American communists of the time, supported their right to trample on the rights of others for the benefit of pursuing the long-term goal of establishing a classless society.

But by the 1920s, Cahan and the *Forward* had changed positions. Cahan had been to Europe and seen what the communists were up to. His experiences there, along with stories of communist "show trials" (trials where political opponents were forced to confess to invented crimes against the state) turned him into an anticommunist. Consequently, the *Forward* began printing vivid accounts of Soviet atrocities and human-rights violations. These stories alienated some of its more radical left-wing readership but brought it more into the mainstream of American journalism.

Of course, the *Forward* was not the only longtime success story in American Yiddish journalism. Another notable publication was the *Day,* which generally was written in a more refined Yiddish style than the *Forward.* This publication, which is

American Jewish Archives

The 1917 Russian Revolution, as depicted in the above postcard, had a political impact in North America as well.

CHAPTER EIGHT:

Jews in North American Theater

The Yiddish Theater

Along with the growth of a vibrant Yiddish press, the Lower East Side gave birth to a vital new theater movement: the Yiddish theater. Beginning in the 1880s, as soon as the Lower East Side reached the critical population mass that made it a Jewish community, theaters began to spring up everywhere in this section of Manhattan.

The Jewish appetite for theater soon proved to be all but unquenchable. Plays were put on every night of the week. As well as evening performances, there were matinees on weekends. At its height, it was estimated that weekly Lower East Side attendance at the theater was close to fifty thousand.

The very first Yiddish play performed was an operetta called *The Sorceress*, which was presented August 12, 1882. Written by Abraham Goldfaden, a European Jewish composer (he later wrote the famous song "Raisins and Almonds"), this first show wasn't much—there was no script, and the players performed what they could remember of productions they had put on in Europe—but it was the start of something big. Within the year, shows were being put on every weekend at a place called the Bowery Garden. Soon after, plays were performed every night.

The Yiddish theater generally eschewed subtle theatrical messages in favor of melodrama and heavy doses of sentimentality.

The necessity of presenting a constant stream of new plays to keep audiences satisfied meant that along with some inspired moments of theater, a lot of schlock found its way onto the Yiddish stage. The two leading impresarios who wrote and produced show after show for the Jews of the Lower East Side were Morris Horowitz, ensconced at a theater called the Romanian Opera House, and Joseph Lateiner, whose company presented its pieces at the Oriental Theater.

These two tireless playwrights adapted Shakespeare, biblical stories, Ibsen, Strindberg, Goethe, and whatever other tales they could get their hands on and put together Yiddish versions for their audiences. When imagination lagged, they even borrowed from each other. If one ran a successful production of a biblical tale, the other soon followed with a similar play.

As a rule in these productions, subtlety was out and melodramatic spectacle was in. Songs about home, motherhood, and the plight of the Jews were often tossed out of context into plays that were unrelated to these subjects. Certain ingredients, demanded by the audience, could not be neglected. When one company put on a Yiddish version of Ibsen's *A Doll's House* (the story of how a woman, Nora, is forced to abandon her husband and family), the actors added an extra act wherein Nora came back to her husband and lived happily ever after. This violated the spirit of the play, but the Lower East Side crowd insisted that plays had to uphold their belief in the inviolability of the Jewish family.

The stars of the theater became larger-than-life personalities. These performers included Madame Liptzin, Zelig Mogolescu, David Kessler, and Bertha Kalisch.

Two of the leading lights of the Yiddish theater were Jacob Adler and Boris Thomashefsky. Thomashefsky had been in the very first production of *The Sorceress*. It was said that no matter what a play was about, Thomashefsky "always managed to get in a song about Mama." And the song always brought the audience to tears.

When they walked about the streets of the East Side, these actors were as mobbed as modern-day movie stars. According to Abraham Cahan, when Jacob Adler strolled down East Broadway in New York, people's faces shone "with adoration, enchantment, and awe."

New York was not the only scene of a thriving Yiddish theater. In Chicago, a theater called Glickman's catered to a Jewish audience. In Philadelphia, there were Yiddish productions at the Standard, the National, and the Arch Street theaters. In Canada, there were three theater groups putting on shows in Montreal as well as productions going on in Toronto and Winnipeg.

When some of the Yiddish theater producers were attacked for the low quality of their productions, they responded, as television producers would respond six decades later, that they were just giving the audiences the kind of drama they wanted. A critic of the time complained, for instance, that Joseph Lateiner's plays had neither "form or ideas.... They are mainly mixed melodrama, broad burlesque, and comic opera." But no matter what the critics thought, the Lower East Siders filled the house night after night.

Abraham Jewish Archives

Abraham Goldfaden wrote the first Yiddish play performed in North America—*The Sorceress*.

American Jewish Archives

Jacob Ben-Ami performed for the Yiddish Art Theater.

Whatever their shortcomings, Lateiner's shows at the Lower East Side's Oriental Theater were designed to be vehicles in which Boris Thomashefsky could show off his talent for emoting. The writer Hutchins Hapgood observed that Lateiner's main characters "are all intended for…Thomashesky, a young man, fat, with curling black hair, languorous eyes, and a rather effeminate voice…[who] picturesquely stands in the middle of the stage and declaims phlegmatically the hero and satisfies the 'romantic' demand of the audience."

The flamboyant course of the Yiddish theater was changed by Jacob Gordin, a Russian émigré who came to New York in 1891. Soon after he arrived, Gordin, who had never even seen a Yiddish play before living on the Lower East Side, decided to write plays that were more conventional and mainstream than the "vulgar, false, and immoral" productions he saw in New York.

Gordin's first staged production, *Siberia,* was dramatically different from the usual Yiddish show. The story of a Russian Jew exiled to Siberia, the play tells how its hero escapes from banishment, finds a new life as a successful businessman, and then is rearrested after being betrayed by an informer. The play did not do very well, because much of the Jewish audience did not know what to make of it. But it was enough of a success to get Gordin started.

Within a decade, Gordin was considered the dominant Yiddish playwright. He, too, borrowed freely from other sources—Shakespeare, Goethe, Ibsen, and so on—but rather than using these sources to create melodramatic vehicles for overblown emoting by egocentric actors, he used classical themes to create a didactic theater focused on the serious concerns of the Lower East Side inhabitants. For example, one of his biggest successes was *De Yiddisher Kenig Lear,* which used Shakespeare's tale of King Lear to teach lessons about bringing up children in the dawn of the twentieth century.

In Gordin's version of Lear, the patriarch of the story is David Masheles, a Russian who is scorned by his children after he gives them all of his wealth. Although Gordin was criticized for stealing from Shakespeare, he had one of the characters in *Kenig Lear* actually warn Masheles of his probable disaster by reciting the plot of the original *Lear.* So the play became not only a warning about unruly offspring, it also tried to teach its audience about literature.

After Gordin died in 1909, serious Yiddish theater quickly died, too. The cost of mounting theatrical productions had risen, and like modern-day Hollywood movie producers looking for blockbusters, Yiddish producers such as Horowitz and Lateiner invested in marquee stars and sensationalist shows with such names as *The Sinner* and *White Slaves* to attract large crowds.

But in 1918, the serious Yiddish theater made a comeback. In that year, the Yiddish Art Theater, led by Maurice Schwartz at the Irving Place Theater in New York, put on a show called *A Secluded Corner,* which had been written by Peretz Hirschbein. The company, which included the actors Ludwig Satz, Bertha Gersten, Jacob Ben-Ami, and Celia Adler, found immediate success. *A Secluded Corner*

American Jewish Archives

American Jewish Archive

ran for three months—which was considered a lengthy run in those days. The company went on to do other serious shows and stimulate a rebirth of legitimate Yiddish theater.

Other important plays at this time were put on by a theatrical company called Artef. Originally established to advocate communist and socialist ideas onstage, the company's work surpassed those restrictive parameters. As it evolved, Artef became a kind of Yiddish avant-garde theater and put on works by Chaver Paver, David Bergelson, and Moshe Nadir. Its innovative style meant that it never attracted a large Jewish downtown crowd, but it did succeed in attracting the attention of mainstream American intellectuals who attended its English-language productions.

By the end of the 1930s, the dispersal of the Lower East Side population, as more and more Jews moved out and assimilated into mainstream American culture, finally doomed the Yiddish theater for the last time. Audiences shrank. The most gifted actors and actresses didn't have to stay on the Lower East Side to find

In 1918, the smash hit *A Secluded Corner* by Maurice Schwartz (above, left) stimulated a rebirth of legitimate Yiddish theater. Jacob Gordin (above, right) enjoyed fantastic success writing plays for the Yiddish theater.

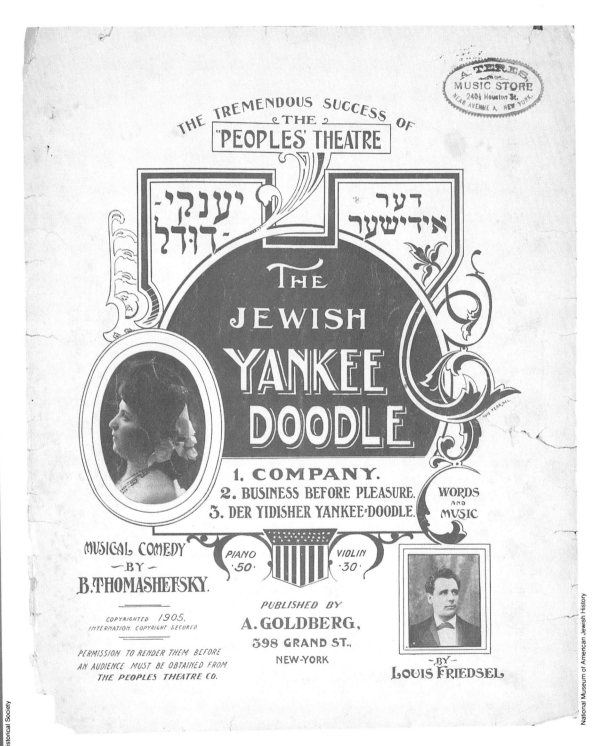

At the height of his popularity, Boris Thomashefsky was well-paid for his starring roles in such shows as *The Green Millionaire* and *The Jewish Yankee Doodle.* But by the late 1930s, Thomashefsky was broke and out of work, singing for his supper in cabarets.

work. They spoke English and took their acts on the road or found work on Broadway or in Hollywood.

Old-timers like Boris Thomashefsky, who had lived it up during the good times and hadn't bothered to invest their money wisely, now found themselves out of work and in serious financial straits. Some were destitute. Thomashefsky, who had made a small fortune as one of the Yiddish theater's biggest stars, had to find work as a singer in cabarets.

In 1920, there had been at least a dozen Yiddish theaters in New York. By the time World War II started, they were practically extinct.

But the end of the Yiddish theater wasn't the end of Jews on the stage. Aside from all the performers who went into vaudeville and invaded the movies (as producers, actors, directors, and so on), there were serious Jewish playwrights and directors who found a place in the legitimate American theater.

One of the most important Jewish-American playwrights to emerge from this era was Clifford Odets. (Some consider him to be the most important.) Odets, born in Philadelphia but raised in New York, wrote plays with a social conscience. His first success, *Waiting for Lefty*, written in 1935, derived its subject matter from a New York taxi drivers' strike that took place the year before.

Odets was called the poet of Jewish-American life. Other Jewish playwrights of the time, such as George S. Kaufman, Moss Hart, and Lillian Hellman, used some of their experiences as American Jews in their work, but Odets relied on it. His other successes include the plays *Awake and Sing!* and *Golden Boy*.

In the 1930s, at the same time as Odets was writing his social realism, a company called the Group Theatre was revolutionizing the conventions of acting and directing. Spearheaded by Harold Clurman and Lee Strasberg, this group emphasized "method" acting. They encouraged actors to improvise on a role to further explore a character's actions and motivations. They also urged actors to use their own life experiences to enhance their performances.

All of these revolutions in performance and directing are still evident in the theater today. Many of today's performers would be lost without these techniques and ideas. And at any time of day, Americans, Canadians, and citizens of almost any country in the world can turn on their televisions or go to the movies or attend a play and see the evidence of these theatrical influences for themselves.

Archives, Jewish Federation of Greater Toronto

The Yiddish theater also flourished in Canada. This poster advertises a show in Toronto in 1928.

CHAPTER NINE

Jewish-American Show Business Goes Beyond the Jewish Community

The Birth of the Film Business

There's no denying that Jews played a dominant, perhaps a predominant, role in the birth of the motion-picture industry in America at the turn of the century. Why this occurred is not easily answered. The early stages of the film industry resembled an amoeba. The geographical and social origins of American film directors, producers, distributors, and actors who went into this lucrative new business represented a disorganized polyglot; its members came from everywhere, including Europe. But as the filmmaking community took shape and established itself in Hollywood, California, making Tinseltown the movie capital of the world, Jewish filmmakers took their place as some of its leading citizens.

AP/Wide World Photos

In the 1920s and 1930s, studio bosses like Louis B. Mayer (left) wielded immense power in Hollywood. Accompanying Mayer to a film premiere are Vera-Ellen (center), and Maureen O'Hara (right).

It is safe to say that none of the men who would go on to form the powerful Hollywood film studios in the first half of the twentieth century planned on entering the filmmaking industry when they were youngsters. At that time, of course, during the last throes of the nineteenth century, there simply was no such industry. Many of these men who later came to power in filmmaking were restless immigrants who had moved from town to town, changing occupations almost as often as they changed clothes.

For example, Louis B. Mayer was born in Minsk, Russia, in 1885. His parents moved to North America when Mayer was young, and he was brought up in St. John, New Brunswick, in Canada. His first job was working for his father as a ship salvager. In 1907, he went into business for himself and bought a movie theater in Haverhill, Massachusetts.

Soon Mayer had his own booking agency, which distributed films in New England. In 1912, he became a naturalized U.S. citizen. In 1914, he began to make a lot of money with the D. W. Griffith film *Birth of a Nation,* for which he had purchased exclusive distribution rights in New England. In 1924, by then living in California, he was the head of production for the MGM Corporation, one of the most powerful movie studios. With this company, even during the worst times of the Great Depression, Mayer was known to take home more than a million dollars a year.

Other Jewish success stories in the cinema business are similar. Before he struck it rich as the head of Universal Pictures, Carl Laemmle had traveled on a personal odyssey over much of North America. He was born in Laupheim, Germany, in 1867. After he immigrated to New York, he worked as a furrier. Then he moved to Chicago and took on odd jobs and later worked on a farm in the Dakotas. After going into the motion-picture business in California, he eventually produced one of the first pictures that cost a million dollars to make: *The Hunchback of Notre Dame.*

But perhaps the most famous of all the early Hollywood producers was Samuel Goldwyn, whose liberties with the English language ("A verbal agreement ain't worth the paper it's written on") made him notorious. Born Schmuel Gelbfisz in 1882 in the Jewish ghetto of Warsaw, Poland, he came to the United States in 1896. A glove salesman in New York before he began to produce plays on Broadway, he saw the possibilities in movies and convinced his brother-in-law, Jesse Lasky, to bankroll his entry into motion pictures.

In 1913, the Lasky Feature Play Company produced its first picture, *The Squaw Man.* Soon, Goldwyn formed the Goldwyn Pictures Corporation. He later joined forces with Louis Mayer to form MGM. Goldwyn is generally credited with being the first Hollywood producer to bring famous authors from New York out to California to write motion-picture scripts. The writers frequently and loudly complained about Goldwyn's pedestrian tastes in scripts, but few could resist the big money he offered to come to Hollywood and work for his company, Eminent Authors, Inc.

AP/Wide World Photos

While the American public adored pre–World War II movie stars like Mickey Rooney (second from left) and Ava Gardner (right), studio heads like Louis B. Mayer (left) held ultimate control over their careers. Second from right is Rooney's mother, shown at the star's twenty-first birthday party.

Carl Laemmle was born in Laupheim, Germany, and worked in odd jobs in New York, South Dakota, and Chicago before becoming a Hollywood magnate. He produced *The Hunchback of Notre Dame,* one of the first movies with a million-dollar budget.

FPG International

Museum of Modern Art

By 1925, when this picture of Sam Goldwyn and his family was taken, Goldwyn, a former glove salesman, was well-established in Hollywood.

FPG International

In Hollywood, Jewish performers as well as Jewish executives found success and riches making films. **Al Jolson (left)** and **Eddie Cantor (seated, right)** were Jewish vaudevillians who became movie stars. **Samuel Goldwyn (right)** was one of the most successful movie producers in history. Also shown here are **Douglas Fairbanks (seated, left)**, **Mary Pickford**, and **Ronald Coleman (standing, second from right)**.

Getting In on the Beginning of Motion Pictures

In the nascent business of filmmaking, everyone was a newcomer, and some historians attribute the early Jewish entree into the filmmaking world to this newness. There was no established elite ready to exclude Jewish businessmen, no industry associations or monopolies set up to slow or prevent the entrance of newcomers, and few established businessmen could foresee its potential. All of the early filmmakers were recent immigrants to the strange, new world of celluloid.

The fact that so many Jews were involved in designing, making, and marketing clothing may have given them an advantage in the early days of motion pictures. Kevin Brownlow, a film historian, points out that early movie moguls like Goldwyn had at some point in their early lives worked in the Lower East Side garment industry. With its focus on following trends in fashion and changes in public taste, the clothing business was an excellent training ground for film executives whose survival depended on keeping abreast of what American (and worldwide) audiences wanted to see in their neighborhood movie theaters.

Jewish businessmen also found that at the turn of the century getting into the movie business was not expensive. For a modest investment, they could purchase nickelodeons—simple machines in which customers dropped a nickel, stared into a narrow viewer, and were treated to a silent movie—and then rent a storefront, install their little machines, and go into business. Quite often, the nickelodeons did great business on the Lower East Side and in other Jewish neighborhoods. The new immigrants were as crazy about watching movies as they were enthusiastic about going to the Yiddish theater.

As motion-picture technology progressed, owning movie theaters was only a small step up from nickelodeons. By 1908, New York City had more than ten dozen movie theaters. More than a third of these were on the Lower East Side.

When Jews started moving into Hollywood and the surrounding California communities in large numbers (not only the producers were Jewish, many of the actors, editors, directors, and cameramen were Jewish, too), the local Presbyterian inhabitants were not happy. But because the industry was dominated by Jews, the local anti-Semitism was short-lived.

Some historians believe that the low cost of entering the movie business in the early 1900s allowed Jewish businessmen their entree into moviemaking. Harry Cohn, head of Columbia Studios, seated here with Rita Hayworth, was one of many Jewish entrepreneurs who found gold in the land of the silver screen.

Movies and Jewish Consciousness

Despite the fact that Jews were involved in so many aspects of the filmmaking business, the portrayal of Jews in the movies was not often forthright. Jews were frequently ignored, because for the most part, moviemakers were not interested

American Jewish Archives

Adolph Zukor, head of Paramount Pictures, was taken aback at the success of the movie *Humoresque*. He thought audiences would be alienated by its focus on poverty and the difficulties of immigrant life in North America.

in promoting social issues or examining their ethnic identity on the screen. They were interested in making money.

In one famous story, Harry Cohn, head of Columbia Pictures, was reputed to have turned an actor down for a role because he looked "too Jewish." When told that the actor was very talented, Cohn (himself Jewish) supposedly replied, "Around here, the only Jews we put into the movies play Indians." In that way, Cohn managed to prove his insensitivity to two ethnic groups with one sentence.

Despite the absence of Jewish ethnic consciousness in much of the product that came out of the film industry, there were some notable exceptions. According to Kevin Brownlow, "If any man could be said to have depicted the sufferings of the Jewish people on celluloid, it was a Russian Jew called Sidney Goldin."

Goldin was born in Odessa, Russia, in 1880. He got started in show business at an early age, and by the time he was fifteen, he was acting in the Yiddish theater in Baltimore. In 1913, he made a three-reel film for Imp Studios (then located in Fort Lee, New Jersey) called *The Sorrows of Israel*. This film was designed to appeal to Lower East Side movie-goers. It depicted the plight of Russian Jews besieged by pogroms and anti-Semitism and pressured to convert to Christianity. Instead of succumbing, the characters in the movie persevered and made their way to America. The movie did well enough to inspire other producers to make more movies about Russian Jews.

In 1913, Goldin made a film called *The Black Hundred*, which detailed the savage pogroms that were taking place in Russia. (The Black Hundred was an anti-Semitic group that killed thousands of Jews.) Jacob Adler starred in the movie as Mendel Beilis, a Russian Jew accused of the ritual murder of a Christian. The charge wasn't true, but as in real life, the on-screen Black Hundred used the accusation as a rationale for attacking more Jews.

While *The Black Hundred* did not make much money, it did a good business on the Lower East Side. And when it was shown in London, its anti-Russian tone raised the hackles of the Russian Embassy.

Sidney Goldin went on to collaborate with Boris Thomashefsky in the filming of some of the plays that Thomashefsky had starred in before packed houses in New York. Apparently, the movie versions of these were failures. Goldin, however, did other films with stars of the Yiddish theater. In 1923, he made a movie in Austria called *East and West*, which starred Molly Picon and her husband, Jacob Kalich, two Lower East Side stars (the movie was released in North America as *Mazel Tov*). He also made a movie with Maurice Schwartz of the Yiddish Art Theater called *Yizkor*.

All of these early movies by Goldin were silent. Toward the end of his life, Goldin did make some Yiddish movies with sound. He died of a heart attack in 1937 at age fifty-seven.

Aside from Goldin's work, there are three early motion pictures that seem to summarize Hollywood's perspective on the North American Jewish experience.

The first of these is *Humoresque,* which Kevin Brownlow calls the first Jewish classic. Financed by William Randolph Hearst, this movie, taken from a short story by the Jewish writer Fannie Hurst, is a sentimental, four-hankie affair about a Jewish musician who suffers an injury and "may never play the violin again."

Filmed in 1920, *Humoresque* takes place on the Lower East Side and features location shots of street life in downtown New York. The plot centers on Leon Kantor, a son of Jewish immigrants who aspires to be a violinist despite his parents' impecunious circumstances. He succeeds at becoming a famous musician, but at the height of his career, he joins the army to fight in World War I. A shrapnel wound paralyzes his arm, but his love for his mother inspires a complete recovery.

Hearst thought the picture was too realistic and depressing and didn't want to release it. Adolph Zukor, the head of Paramount Pictures and himself Jewish, agreed that the movie focused too much on poor Jews rather than "Rothschilds, banks, and beautiful things."

But apparently Paramount needed a movie to fill in the gap between two bookings, and so it debuted the film with no fanfare or publicity. To the studio's surprise, the movie did booming business. In New York, *Humoresque* played for twelve weeks and set a box office record.

On the plus side, *Humoresque* proved that film-goers liked their movies spiced with some gritty realism (as long as good triumphed over evil). So other filmmakers went ahead and made movies that had some sparks of real life. On the negative side, this film caused filmmakers to load their films with plenty of sentimentality. Instead of spoonfuls of sweet sentiment, directors poured it on by the bucketful.

Sentimentality certainly plays a large role in *The Jazz Singer,* a 1927 film concerned with the Jewish experience. This movie, the first with sound, tells the story of the son of a cantor who goes into show business and falls in love with a gentile girl, but in the end, the son comes back to take his father's place in the synagogue, singing during Yom Kippur services.

While *The Jazz Singer* is intensely melodramatic and a bit overwrought for modern tastes, it does try to deal with the problem of Jewish assimilation into American society. The movie stars Al Jolson, a Jewish vaudeville entertainer who was one of the most popular singers of his time. Born as Asa Yoelson, Jolson had changed his name to fit into mainstream American show business, and in fact, the movie's story line mirrors some of his own experience.

As may be the rule with Hollywood productions, Samson Raphaelson was appalled by the film, which had been based on his play, *The Jazz Singer.* He called the motion picture a "dreadful picture…very few worse," but audiences still loved it. And technologically, the new Vitaphone process that provided the sound for the songs and occasional dialogue meant the beginning of the end of silent pictures.

The movie *Abie's Irish Rose* also deals with the assimilation of Jews into American society. Based on a stage play that was incredibly popular, this comedic film

FPG International

Al Jolson, a Jewish vaudeville performer who had changed his name from Asa Yoelson, found great success as a singer, songwriter, and actor.

AL JOLSON in "THE JAZZ SINGER" with May McAvoy — A Warner Bros. Production

In *The Jazz Singer,* one of the first motion pictures with sound, Al Jolson portrayed a performer torn between his career and his Jewish beliefs. Jolson felt the role mirrored his own early life experiences as a vaudeville performer.

tells the rather inane story of a Jewish husband and Irish wife who tell his parents that they are both Jewish and, at the same time, try to convince her parents that he is Irish. All of the jokes in the movie (and play) derive from that situation.

Although the play had a lengthy run in New York and enjoyed successful tours across North America, the movie bombed. The stage version had reportedly earned its author, Anne Nichols (who wasn't Jewish) more than eight million dollars. Unable to understand the movie's failure, studio executive Jesse Lasky said, "I can't understand why it [the movie] didn't do phenomenal business, since the picture was every bit as bad as the play."

The Jews in Vaudeville and Beyond

At the same time that filmmaking was developing into a big business, Jewish entrepreneurs were helping to build a network of theatrical bookers, performers, actors, singers, songwriters, and comedians that would have a huge influence on American entertainment for the rest of the twentieth century.

Here, too, on the live stage, Jews seemed to fill a gap that the rest of established America was not prepared to fill. From the streets of the Lower East Side, Brooklyn, and other Jewish neighborhoods across the continent, Jewish kids worked up their acts and took them on the road. And often it was Jewish booking agents who hired them for engagements.

At one point in the early 1900s, two Jews, Marc Klaw and Abraham Erlanger, developed an entertainment syndicate that monopolized vaudeville bookings in theaters across the country. Almost all of the show-business acts had to book through them until Samuel, Jacob, and Lee Shubert set up their own New York–based theater monopoly and fought the syndicate. They were so successful at beating the syndicate at its own game that historians estimate that at the height of the Shuberts' success, two out of three theater tickets purchased in America were bought from these three brothers.

The acts that went on tour often got started as bands of street performers. For instance, George Burns first performed as part of a singing foursome called the Pee Wee Quartette. Street corners and barrooms were their training ground. In the parks of New York, Burns and others taught each other dance steps. Then Burns got a job as a dance instructor at Bennie Bernstein's Dancing School on the Lower East Side. After that, he started in vaudeville, eventually putting together comedy routines with Gracie Allen. Later, Burns and Allen would have their own television show.

Eddie Cantor got started in much the same fashion, doing shticks (routines) on the Lower East Side, singing schmaltzy songs, passing the hat, and scratching out a living. When a friend of his, Roy Arthur, who was working on the vaudeville stage, started to go legit—with a band of jugglers—he got Cantor an audition that led to Cantor's first vaudeville engagement.

After getting his start on New York's Lower East Side, Eddie Cantor (above, right) tried his hand at many forms of entertainment—he even did commercials for NBC.

IRVING BERLIN

*God Bless America
Land that I love
Stand beside her
And guide her
Through the night with a light
From above
From the mountains
To the prairies
To the ocean
White with foam
God Bless America
My home sweet home.*

Irving Berlin

Songs like Berlin's "God Bless America" cause many to view Berlin as the leading American composer of all time.

Library of Congress

The Jewish performers of the time made great use of Yiddish and traditional Jewish culture for both laughs and tear-jerking sentimentality. Sophie Tucker relied on the song "My Yiddishe Mama" to make the audience grab for its handkerchiefs. The Marx Brothers, Cantor, Burns, George Jessel—they all made fun of the old Jewish men they had known all their lives and parodied the over-protective Jewish mother.

They went to great lengths to secure bookings. The agent A. J. Balaban reported that there was a Jewish group everywhere imitating some ethnic group or other. While negotiating a fee with a Hawaiian band whose leader insisted they had just traveled thousands of miles from the Pacific, Balaban tossed a question at the bandleader in Yiddish. As Balaban recalled, the musician answered in Yiddish, "in a natural New Yorker's tone, without a trace of a Hawaiian accent. We quickly came to terms, complimenting him on his ability to impersonate."

Along with Hawaiian imitations and Yiddish routines, the performers imitated the Irish, the Italians (Chico Marx relied on his well-developed imitation of an Italian immigrant), the Germans, and any other kind of American they could find.

The co-opting of all these ethnic identities wasn't just the province of the comedians. Songwriters also used it to great success. Irving Berlin, perhaps the greatest American songwriter of all time, incorporated various ethnic "impersonations" in many of his early hits.

Berlin, who was born Israel Baline (everyone in the old neighborhood called him Izzy), got his start as a singing waiter at a restaurant in New York's Chinatown. The first song that he sold to a publisher was "Marie From Sunny Italy," an ersatz Italian tune for which he and his collaborator earned the grand total of thirty-six cents. After losing his day job, he wrote "Sadie Salome," a ditty about a Jewish girl who abandons her straitlaced fiancé for a career in vaudeville, and he penned the Irish-style tune "I Wish That You Was My Gal Molly." His song "Dorando" was from an Italian point of view, and his first monster hit, "Alexander's Ragtime Band," was a blackface song that parodied the ragtime tunes that African Americans were writing.

Curiously enough, blackface performing was an important ingredient in Jewish performers' routines in the first part of the twentieth century. When Sophie Tucker played in New York City, she headlined as "The Manipulator of Coon Melodies" (in the less refined rural areas of the country, the billing proclaimed her a "World Renowned Coon Shouter"). With burned cork smeared all over her face and wearing a white satin dress, she belted out songs as if she were an African-American.

Those were simpler (and more overtly racist) times, and for the most part, the audiences were unsophisticated. Tucker wore gloves during her act, and when she finished, she doffed the gloves and held up her lily-white hands. Many people in the audiences were shocked to find they had been listening to a "white girl."

One of Sophie Tucker's biggest hits was "My Yiddishe Mama." By the end of the tune, there wasn't a dry eye in the house.

On stage as well as on the silver screen, the Marx Brothers' frenetic style of anarchistic comedy wowed audiences. Here (from left) Harpo, Groucho, and Chico are caught in a rare somnolent moment.

Museum of Modern Art

Library of Congress (Gershwin+Berlin Photo)

George Gershwin (above, left) and Irving Berlin were two composers whose creativity and genius have exerted tremendous impact on American music.

AP/Wide World Photos

Itzhak Perlman, the Israel Philharmonic's solo violinist, is one of the world's premier musicians.

Leonard Bernstein displayed his talent as a conductor and classical composer as well as a writer of hit Broadway musicals, including *West Side Story*.

Following on the heels of Berlin, George and Ira Gershwin took elements of popular music (especially African-American innovations), combined them with the structure of classical music, and set the musical community on its heels with new compositions. In particular, George Gershwin's composition "Rhapsody in Blue" changed the direction of modern, classical American music, opening it up to jazz motifs and melodic variations. And after it was recorded and exported to Europe, Gershwin's work influenced composers and music listeners around the world.

Of course, although the Eastern European immigrants played the major role in all of these Jewish-influenced changes in the North American performing arts, they were not by any means the only ones taking part. Jerome Kern, for example, was an influential musician and composer from a German-Jewish background. Born in 1885, Kern's major contribution was the score for the musical *Show Boat*. Collaborating on the show with Oscar Hammerstein, Kern wrote the song, "Ol' Man River," a tune that for many years symbolized the repressed feelings and oppressed lives of African-Americans to many white liberals. (Of course, today, the same song appears to symbolize almost the opposite—its sentiment captures a kind of Uncle Tom obsequiousness.)

In addition to her enormously successful singing career, Barbra Streisand (right) is also one of the most powerful actresses and producers in Hollywood. In 1902, Jacob Epstein (above) illustrated the book *The Spirit of the Ghetto*. He used the proceeds to finance his art education in Europe. Epstein was later knighted in Great Britain. Jo Davidson (opposite, top right) is one of the most well-known Jewish sculptors. His outspoken personality has made Norman Mailer (opposite, bottom right) a well-known celebrity as well as an accomplished author. Playwright Neil Simon (opposite, left) is one of the best-known dramatists of our time.

Kern also collaborated with Hammerstein on the shows *Sally*, *Sunny*, and *Roberta*, and he wrote the songs "Smoke Gets in Your Eyes," "The Last Time I Saw Paris," and "Can't Help Lovin' Dat Man."

The list of North American Jewish contributors to all areas of show business and the arts is long and varied. Musicians include Benny Goodman, Jascha Heifetz, and Itzhak Perlman as well as the classical composers Aaron Copeland and Leonard Bernstein, pop composers Bob Dylan and Paul Simon, and the singers Barbra Streisand, Beverly Sills, and Art Garfunkel. Actors include Paul Muni, Shelley Winters, Kirk Douglas, the Marx Brothers, Jack Benny, Edward G. Robinson, and Dustin Hoffman. In the field of drama and film, there are dramatists Arthur Miller and Neil Simon as well as the directors Steven Spielberg, Richard Benjamin, Carl and Rob Reiner, and Woody Allen.

In the fine arts, Sir Jacob Epstein, Jo Davidson, and Louise Nevelson are outstanding Jewish sculptors. Max Weber, Mark Rothko, Larry Rivers, and Ben Shahn are a few of the most gifted Jewish painters. Isaac B. Singer, Bernard Malamud, Saul Bellow, Philip Roth, and Norman Mailer are among the most distinguished writers of this century.

American Jewish Archives

AP/Wide World Photos

AP/Wide World Photos

Jewish gangsters Meyer Lansky (left) and Benjamin (Bugsy) Siegel (right)
were the first to see the lucrative possibilities in creating a gambling oasis
in Las Vegas.

CHAPTER TEN

Famous—and Infamous—Jewish Americans of the Twentieth Century

The Jewish Gangsters

It would have been nothing short of miraculous had a poor, overpopulated community like the Jewish Lower East Side produced labor unions, show-business types, musicians, land-lords, doctors, lawyers, writers, newspapermen, furriers, and so on and not been the birth-place of at least a few criminals. Naturally enough, this turbulent era did spawn its share of colorful crime figures.

AP/Wide World Photos

For a short time in the 1930s, gangster Louis Amberg (above) and his bootlegging brothers ruled the Brooklyn underworld. A gang war, won by Louis Lepke, destroyed them.

The first Jewish gangsters probably originated in the gangs that formed on the busy streets. The Irish had their own gangs protecting their turf, the Italians banded together to defend their neighborhoods, and the Jews did likewise. Then, just as the workers in the sweatshops joined together to form large and powerful labor unions, the more ambitiously unlawful kids and young men of the Lower East Side graduated from petty thievery to more lucrative forms of crime and corruption and joined together to form criminal syndicates and the "mob."

One of the most notorious of these gangsters was Abe Reles, who grew up to be a key figure in Murder, Inc., a group of criminals who specialized in killings for hire. As a child, Reles was described by a policeman who patrolled the Brownsville section of Brooklyn as "...mean and tough.... He used to slap the younger boys around, take their nickels from them, break up their little homemade carts."

Frustrated with school and his after-school job, Reles dropped out of legitimate society and got a job as an "enforcer" for a bootlegging mob run by the Amberg brothers—Joe, Louis, Hymie, and Oscar. At the time, the Brooklyn-based Amberg gang was relatively small potatoes in the New York crime world when compared to the more powerful group run by the infamous Louis Lepke, but Reles figured he could start with the Ambergs and work his way up over the bodies of others.

Reles' first big break came when Lepke ordered the Ambergs to rub out the Shapiro brothers, who were muscling in on Lepke's garment-center protection racket. The Ambergs passed the job on to Reles, who relished his assignment. One of his most well-known "hits" was when he took Willie Shapiro, who was only seventeen years old, and buried him alive in a Canarsie swamp.

When Lepke decided he could live without the Ambergs, he hired Reles to rub out his own bosses. Reles was only too happy to oblige. Soon he was ruling Brownsville.

It didn't last long. As might be expected, the brutal Lepke eventually decided he'd had enough of Reles, too. Realizing his life expectancy was short, Reles turned himself in to the authorities and described the inner workings of Murder, Inc., to district attorney William O'Dwyer. But Reles never got to testify in court. While in police custody, he fell (or was thrown) from a fifth-floor window.

After Reles died, kids in his old neighborhood of Brownsville tore the place apart. It was rumored that Reles had hidden about $75,000 in a "safe place." The money was never found, although it's quite possible that if anyone dug it up, they never told.

Lepke, the man who ordered Reles' death (and the deaths of so many others), was the product of a broken home on the Lower East Side. His original name was Louis Buchalter. This fearsome psychopath got the name Lepke from a nickname his mother used to call him: Lepkeleh (which means, literally, "little Louis").

Lepke showed true criminal genius when he came up with the concept of applying strong-arm tactics to unions and the garment industry and milking this business for millions year after year. He started off as a thug who kept unhappy union mem-

Believing his pals had marked him for death, mobster and murderer Abe Reles (above, left) decided to turn stool pigeon and give evidence against his comrades in crime. It didn't save him. In 1941, while he was in police custody, he took a fatal dive out a hotel window. His murder was never solved.

AP/Wide World Photos

bers in line for corrupt union bosses. Pretty soon, he and his henchmen were breaking heads and throwing acid in people's faces. He installed puppet union officers who followed his directions. He skimmed union dues and took payoffs from factory owners in exchange for labor peace. By taking over organizations of truck drivers, bakery workers, projectionists, taxi drivers, and so on, it is estimated that Lepke's organization was raking in at least $100 million a year in the 1930s.

In running this vast enterprise, Lepke was meticulous and ruthless. He kept an eye on more than two hundred sources of income at the same time and had hundreds of gangsters (and crooked accountants) working under him. When the going got rough, his motto was, "No witnesses." Those who talked, or threatened to talk, died.

In the end, Lepke's notoriety and the revelations of the late Reles mobilized the authorities against him. (Even though Reles never testified, he did give an earful of informative narrative to O'Dwyer before flying out the window.) When Lepke ordered Max Rubin, a garment-center thug, bumped off, the hit was botched. Rubin survived to give testimony that sent Lepke to the chair.

Jewish crime wasn't restricted to New York. Just as the Jews were the first to see the lucrative potential in the film industry, the Jewish partnership of Bugsy Siegel and Meyer Lansky was the first to see the profitable possibilities in setting up a gambling capital in the Nevada desert.

During the 1930s, Lansky was the financial brains of the mob. (In *The Godfather, Part II,* Lee Strasberg plays a character based on Lansky.). Lansky invented ways to launder gangsters' dirty money so the authorities couldn't find it, and he supervised mob investments in other countries, helped set up profitable operations in Cuba and the Bahamas, and hid money in Swiss bank accounts.

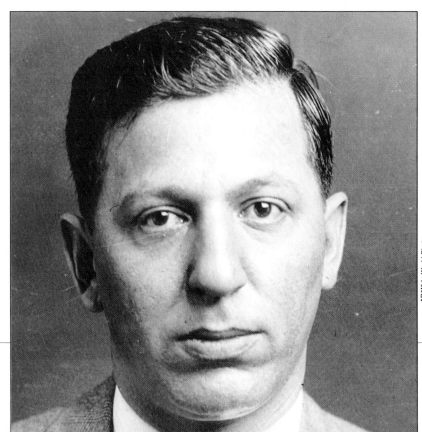

AP/Wide World Photos

AP/Wide World Photos

Meyer Lansky, flanked by policemen (above), makes a rare appearance at a police station. Authorities could rarely make charges against him stick. Louis "Lepke" Buchalter (left and far left) ran a crime empire that terrorized New York's garment district. While Lansky kept a low profile that allowed him to eventually die of old age, Buchalter's notorious brutality helped earn him a one-way trip to the electric chair in 1941.

Albert Michelson (right) was the first American scientist to win the Nobel Prize. One of his designs included a device called the interferometer (opposite), which measured the wavelength of light.

American Jewish Archives

Medicine and Science

Gambling and early investment in Las Vegas wasn't the Jews' only claim to fame in Nevada. Oddly enough, one of the first prominent Jewish-American scientists of Eastern European descent didn't grow up on the Lower East Side of New York. He spent his childhood in Virginia City, Nevada.

Albert Abraham Michelson was born in Strelno, Prussia, in 1852, but his parents left Europe when he was an infant. While his parents lived in New York City for a short time, his father, who had found employment there as a jeweler, left the East and went into the dry-goods business in Nevada. The young Michelson, an excellent student at an early age, also spent time in San Francisco, staying with relatives while he went to school there.

Since his parents were poor, at sixteen, Michelson took the United States Naval Academy entrance examination, his best chance at higher education. Even though he got one of the best scores in the country, he did not secure an appointment. Not to be denied, he traveled alone to Washington, D.C., naively hoping to seek help from President Ulysses S. Grant.

Michelson's two-thousand-mile trip across the country wasn't in vain. In Washington, he waylaid Grant while the president was walking his dog (presidents were less insulated in those days) and talked Grant into giving him an executive appointment to the academy. This decision turned out to be one of Grant's better actions during what was to be eight years of otherwise poor presidential judgment.

At the Naval Academy, Michelson shone, placing near or at the top of his class in math, science, optics, and acoustics. He also proved to be a standout fencer, boxer, tennis player, and violinist. About the only thing he couldn't handle was a boat. He was a failure once he was off dry land.

So after graduating from the academy and spending two obligatory, unhappy years at sea, Michelson permanently put into port as an instructor. He taught science at the Naval Academy from 1875 to 1879. While there, he put together a surprisingly simple and ingenious apparatus that accurately measured the speed of light in a vacuum. His brilliant discovery captured worldwide attention.

After resigning from the academy, he went to Europe and studied physics in Berlin, Heidelberg, and Paris. Ever a stickler for precision, in 1880 Michelson designed a device called an interferometer, which established a means of accurately measuring the wavelength of light. Later, he also designed what is called an echelon spectroscope, which enabled astronomers to accurately measure the diameters of the stars.

Michelson is also remembered for his involvement with something he didn't discover: ether, an unmoving, inert, mysterious substance that many nineteenth-century scientists believed filled outer space. In 1887, Michelson and another scientist, Edward William Morley, performed a series of experiments that disproved the existence of this substance.

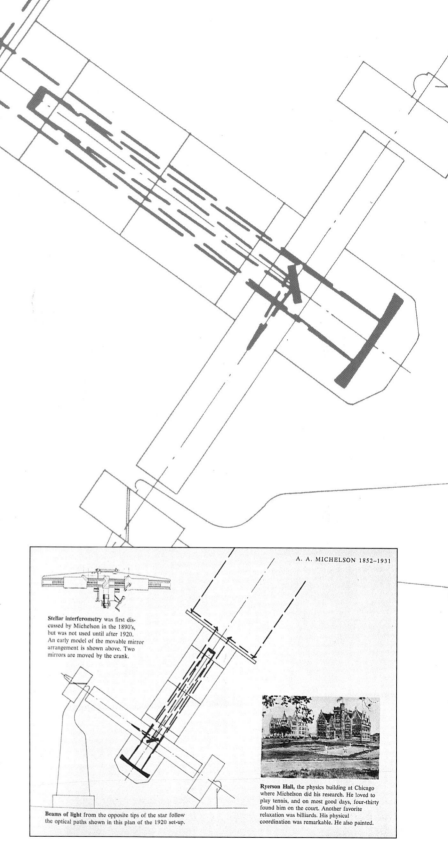

A. A. MICHELSON 1852-1931

Stellar interferometry was first discussed by Michelson in the 1890's, but was not used until after 1920. An early model of the movable mirror arrangement is shown above. Two mirrors are moved by the crank.

Ryerson Hall, the physics building at Chicago where Michelson did his research. He loved to play tennis, and on most good days, four-thirty found him on the court. Another favorite relaxation was billiards. His physical coordination was remarkable. He also painted.

Beams of light from the opposite tips of the star follow the optical paths shown in this plan of the 1920 set-up.

Chicago Jewish Archives/Spertus College

American Jewish Archives

After moving to North America from Germany, Albert Einstein (above) took the oath of a U.S. citizen (opposite). The physicist, who pioneered the theory of relativity, spent many years at Princeton University.

AP/Wide World Photos

Working at the University of Pittsburgh, Dr. Jonas E. Salk developed one of the first polio vaccines.

Albert Michelson, the young man from Virginia City via Prussia and New York, became the first American scientist to win a Nobel Prize, which he received in 1907 for physics. For the last forty years of his life, until just before he died in 1931, Michelson was the head of the physics department at the University of Chicago. The Naval Academy that he had such difficulty entering now has a building—Michelson Hall—named after him.

Albert Einstein, the German Jewish scientist who proposed the influential theory of relativity (and who also emigrated to the United States), credited Michelson's work with making the relativity theory possible. Einstein told Michelson, "It was you who led the physicists into new paths…through your marvelous experimental work…."

While Michelson may be the first name among Jewish-American scientists and doctors, he was by no means the last. The list is long—practically endless. Jonas Salk and Albert Sabin, developers of the first two polio vaccines, are among them. So is Casimir Funk, who did some of the most important biochemical work that extracted vitamins from food and identified them. Joseph Goldberger made nutritional discoveries that led to cures for pellagra, a deficiency disease caused by a lack of niacin that once afflicted many in the southern part of the United States. (Today, many foods, such as bread and white rice, are fortified with niacin and other B vitamins.)

Along with Michelson, many other Jewish-American researchers have won the Nobel Prize, including Konrad Bloch, who made important discoveries concerning cholesterol, and Gerald Edelman, who won for his work in the field of immunology. Surely this list will continue to grow in the future as a new generation of scientists takes their place alongside these pioneers.

American Jewish Archives

Albert Sabin emigrated to the United States from Russia in 1921. He joined the faculty of the College of Medicine at the University of Cincinnati in 1939 and successfully developed a vaccine for immunization against polio in 1959.

132

CHAPTER ELEVEN

Jewish Organizations and the Preservation of Community

Banding Together

Throughout their history in North America, Jews have banded together in community organizations as well as fraternal and sororal groups for three main reasons: to help members of society who need assistance because of poverty or disability, to combat the periodic anti-Semitism that inevitably flares up in virtually all the societies in which Jews have lived throughout their history, and lastly, to aid in the establishment of a homeland for Jews.

Canadian Jewish Congress National Archives

Aaron Hart was one of the first Jewish settlers to live in Canada.

While it's true that North America has generally been free of the virulent anti-Semitism that infected much of the Old World, this never-dying hatred has still made its presence known on this continent. Today, most Jews believe that only a constant vigilance can keep anti-Semitism at bay. Ignoring it and pretending that it doesn't exist won't prevent its reoccurrence. Anti-Semitism has never seemed to die of benign neglect—or any other kind of neglect, for that matter.

Even when Jews were a tiny minority in the New World, anti-Semitism made itself known in North America—long before Jews formed organizations to counteract it. For instance, while Canada has generally been a tolerant society throughout much of its history, this country was not amicable to its Jewish inhabitants from the start. It took longer for Jews to gain full rights in Canada and eliminate Canadian anti-Semitic laws than it took for them to establish citizenship privileges in most of the United States.

Established initially as a French colony, Canada did not even admit Jewish settlers when it was first started. Only French Catholics were welcomed according to the stipulations of the Company of New France, the Gallic enterprise begun in 1627 to supervise French North American colonization.

Despite the rules, Jews slipped into the colony. Because they kept a low profile and few records were kept, no one is precisely sure who the first ones were, but it is known that by the mid-1700s, Abraham Gradis, a Jew from Portugal, had set up a profitable trading company in Quebec. Then, after the British took over Canada, more Jewish settlers moved in. A particularly prominent Jewish colonist from this time was Aaron Hart, a descendant of German Jews who was born in London. He established himself as a successful merchant at a settlement called Trois-Rivières.

Despite the economic prosperity enjoyed by Hart and other Canadian Jews, when Hart's son, Ezekiel, was elected to the Canadian Assembly in 1807, the assembly refused to seat him because he was Jewish. By an overwhelming majority, they voted that all persons "professing the Jewish religion cannot take a seat nor sit nor vote in the House [the Assembly]." When Ezekiel Hart was reelected by the voters of his community, the Canadian Assembly voted the same way all over again, kicking him out because he was Jewish.

At that time, Canada was still closely connected to Great Britain. In 1810, the British government, consulting with the Canadian Assembly, affirmed that they agreed with the Canadian government's anti-Semitic attitude, stating officially that a Jewish representative "could not sit in the Assembly as he could not take an oath upon the Gospels." In the face of this overwhelming official opposition to his career in the government and without any kind of Jewish organization to back him up, Ezekiel Hart gave up the fight and resigned himself to a life as a banker.

Later on, during the War of 1812 when Canada was allied with Great Britain, the Canadian Jews sometimes had great problems serving as officers. One gentile officer claimed, "Christian soldiers would not tolerate a Jew in their midst." Still, some Jews, denied commissions as officers, signed on as enlisted men. Others, despite the opposition of some in the Canadian ruling classes, did manage to serve as lieutenants and captains.

To achieve full rights in Canada, Canadian Jews had to organize themselves and lobby the government again and again.

In the 1820s, Ezekiel Hart's younger brother, Benjamin Hart, picked up the struggle where the rest of the family had left off. He organized the fifty or so Jews living in Montreal and circulated a petition demanding official recognition of the Jewish religion by the Canadian government. Up until this time, there was no official government record keeping of Jewish births, deaths, and marriages. This lack of official records complicated the legal rulings on property owned by Jews and on estates controlled by members of the Jewish community.

Under pressure but not really opposed any longer to recognizing Jews as citizens, the government obliged. In 1831, legal recognition of Judaism as one of the religions of Canada was granted. It is generally believed that the French-Canadian members of the assembly helped pass this kind of legislation recognizing Jews and other non-English religions as part of their campaign to dilute English power in Canada.

However, there was still an obstacle to Jews holding public office—the technicality of having to take oaths for serving in the legislature or as magistrates. Here again, the Hart family took up the struggle. Denied a position as justice of the peace because he wouldn't take a Christian oath, Ezekiel Hart's oldest son, Samuel Becancour Hart, began circulating petitions demanding equal rights for Jews. One was addressed to William IV, king of England. Additionally, Hart and his followers peppered the Canadian Assembly with a steady stream of petitions.

In June of 1832, the Canadian Assembly finally passed "An Act to declare persons professing the Jewish Religion entitled to all the rights and privileges of the other subjects of His Majesty in this Province." This act, while going a long way to granting Jews equal rights, wasn't the end of the battle.

Despite the assembly's intention of granting all rights to Jews, there were still arguments over exactly what kind of an "oath of office" Jews could take to enter public service. Technically, the oaths still demanded true faith to Christianity.

Finally, in 1837, the legislature officially ruled that Jews could assume public office by taking an oath that was personally acceptable to the officeholder. The government would not demand that they express Christian faith. This particular battle for rights in Canada had at last been won. Interestingly enough, it wasn't until almost a quarter of a century later that the Jews in England were granted similar rights.

Anti-Semitism in the United States

Meanwhile, to the south of Canada, the U.S. federal government put its Bill of Rights into force in 1788, which separates affairs of church and state and also guarantees equal rights to all citizens. Religious or ethnic identity was not supposed to

Canadian Jewish Congress National Archives

Ezekiel Hart, Aaron's son, was elected to the Canadian Assembly in 1807, but the Assembly refused to seat him because he was Jewish.

As stated in the resolution above, Jacob Henry was denied a seat in the North Carolina state legislature because of his Jewish faith.

interfere with citizenship rights. As a matter of fact, in the 1788 parade celebrating ratification of this remarkable document, Gershom Mendes Seixas, the cantor of the Shearith Israel congregation in New York, marched with Christian clergy as a symbol of the country's religious pluralism.

But there were still incidents of discrimination. For instance, in 1809, a man named Jacob Henry was denied a seat in the North Carolina state legislature. At that time, the North Carolina state constitution prohibited officeholders from "deny[ing] the being of God or the truth of the Protestant religion...."

When they refused to recognize his status as a legislator, Henry, who had been duly elected, protested vociferously, saying a "man ought to suffer civil disqualifications for what he does and not for what he thinks."

No matter how eloquently he stated his case, the North Carolina constitutional restrictions that stood in his way were left in place. Henry, however, did get to sit in the North Carolina legislature—after he received a special exemption to the rules that barred Jews from the legislature. But it wasn't until nearly sixty years later, in 1868, during Reconstruction after the American Civil War, that the North Carolina constitution was amended to permit Jews to serve as state officials.

Some of the other states also resisted granting full citizenship rights to Jews. One of these was Maryland. Beginning in 1797, Jews and others sympathetic to their cause began to petition the Maryland state government for equal rights for the Jewish community that were denied by the state constitution. But although some in the government thought the Jewish request reasonable in light of the principles of the new country, seven years later, in 1804, the activists were forced to give up their efforts—nothing had been done to rectify the situation.

Then in 1818, the struggle in Maryland began again. Thomas Kennedy, a member of the Maryland legislature, put forward motions to place Maryland's "Jewish inhabitants on equal footing with Christians." There was fierce opposition to Kennedy's "Jew Bill." When the legislature voted on Kennedy's proposal for Jewish equal rights, it went down in defeat—only about a third of the legislature favored it.

In and out of office for the next seven years, Kennedy kept fighting for his principles. Finally, in 1825, the Jews of Maryland were granted full rights under state law. The fight had taken almost thirty years to win equal rights for a population of only about 150 Jews who lived in Maryland at the time. In the whole United States, in 1825, there was an estimated population of about six thousand Jews.

Jewish Organizations

During the period when Jews were fighting for their basic rights, virtually the only Jewish organizations that formally existed were the congregations. Generally, these organizations did not engage in political activities.

The other organizations that first started in the early eighteenth century were not political. They were mostly oriented toward helping the disadvantaged. For example, the Hebrew Benevolent Society was formed in 1820 in New York with this in mind. Originally, this charitable organization started as an effort to care for an impoverished elderly veteran of the Revolutionary War, but the fund-raising was so successful that the members of the society used their resources to continue helping widows, orphans, and disabled members of the community who needed assistance.

Later on, in 1857, Mount Sinai, a Jewish hospital, was formed in New York City. This new institution (which developed into a string of Mount Sinai hospitals up and

Mount Sinai Hospital on West Twenty-Eighth Street in New York City was built in the 1850s.

American Jewish Archives

During much of its history, Mount Sinai Hospital has provided internships for Jewish doctors (such as these early members of its staff) who were discriminated against by many other hospitals.

Courtesy of the Archives of the Mt. Sinai Medical Center

Sampson Simpson founded the Mount Sinai Hospital in New York City.

down the East Coast) had several purposes. The first, of course, was to help the sick. Another reason for the new hospitals was to preserve Jewish identity. It seems that many of the older hospitals were staffed by nuns, and in their overambitious attempts to help the sick, they baptized Jews just before they died so that they would be "saved." This practice, of course, offended Jewish sensibilities and was remedied by caring for sick members of the Jewish community in Jewish hospitals.

The Mount Sinai hospitals also provided internships for Jews who had graduated from medical school, since many of the other hospitals had the anti-Semitic practice of not admitting Jewish graduates.

In 1843, the Independent Order of B'nai B'rith, the initial and probably the most important of the Jewish fraternal orders, was started. Also known as the Sons of the Covenant, this was originally a lodge that admitted only German-American Jews, but the group eventually let in Jews of other origins (and it also did away with the secret rituals, rules, and so on that mark many semisecret societies).

The inaugural meeting of the group took place at a café on New York's Lower East Side. Its first leader was an American Jew with the unlikely name of Henry Jones.

The members of B'nai B'rith saw themselves as mediators in the struggle between the Reform and the Orthodox Jews, bringing together Jews of different walks of life in common philanthropic enterprises.

Within a few years of B'nai B'rith's birth, there were other Jewish fraternal groups: Free Sons of Israel, B'nai Abraham, Kesher Shel Barzel, and B'nai Moishe. Eventually, there were women's organizations, too, including the United Order of True Sisters.

By the 1860s, B'nai B'rith was establishing hospitals and orphanages across the United States. Soon it became an international organization with branches in Canada as well as Europe. At this time there were more than forty B'nai B'rith lodges in North America.

It wasn't until 1913 that B'nai B'rith started the branch called the Anti-Defamation League, formed to fight anti-Semitism. Although the nineteenth century had seen its share of anti-Jewish feelings and activities, this peculiar form of prejudice evolved into a much more ferocious and frightening form of hatred after the twentieth century had begun in earnest.

Anti-Semitic Events That Mobilized the Jewish Community

One of the first well-publicized incidents of American anti-Semitism that elucidated the need for an organized effort at combating anti-Jewish prejudice occurred in 1877. It didn't happen to a poor, recently arrived immigrant who was unfamiliar with America. It happened to one of the United States' most respected

American Jewish Archives

Joseph Seligman, a leading banker of the nineteenth century, created a national furor after being excluded from the Grand Union Hotel in Saratoga, New York, because he was Jewish.

and wealthiest citizens: Joseph Seligman. Seligman was a man who not only lived a life that exemplified the kind of rags-to-riches story that Horatio Alger made famous, he also had Alger on his payroll.

Joseph Seligman, the oldest of eleven children, was born in Bavaria in 1819. His father was a weaver. When he was fourteen, his family scraped together enough money to send Seligman to the University of Erlangen, one of Germany's well-known universities.

By seventeen, Seligman had decided he'd had enough of Europe, and in 1836, he sailed for North America. After landing in New York City, Seligman walked and hitched his way to Mauch Chunk, Pennsylvania (also known as John Thorpe). In Mauch Chunk, he lived with a relative and secured employment with Asa Packer, a builder of coal barges who was destined to make a great fortune from the Lehigh Valley Railroad and also serve as the president of Lehigh University.

Seligman remained a lifelong friend of Packer's, but not his employee. He quit his job with Packer to go into business for himself as a door-to-door peddler in the hills of Pennsylvania. After about a year, he had made enough money to pay for two of his brothers to come across the Atlantic from Europe and join his thriving business.

Within four years, the Seligman brothers' business was doing well enough to rent a headquarters in Lancaster, Pennsylvania. Money went to Bavaria to bring another brother to Pennsylvania. From peddling, the brothers branched out into merchandising from a fixed location.

Soon the Seligmans were selling from stores in Alabama as well as Pennsylvania. Money again was sent to Bavaria. This time the entire family came over (except Seligman's mother, who had already passed away). Most of the family settled on New York's Lower East Side.

While business boomed, the Seligmans often ran into anti-Semitism in their far-flung operations. At one point, Seligman almost went to jail for a fight he got into with a man who insulted the Seligmans' Jewish ancestry.

In 1848, after marrying Babet Steinhart, a woman he had met during a trip to Europe, Seligman settled in New York City and set up the headquarters of what was known as J. & W. Seligman & Company at One William Street. At about the same time as Joseph Seligman was putting down roots in New York, his brother Jesse was in San Francisco running a store and doing a lucrative banking business in the buying and selling of gold bars.

By the time the Civil War started, the Seligmans ran one of the leading banks in the United States and also had branches in Europe. Consequently, they also sold U.S. bonds to Europeans to support the war effort. After the war, when Grant was elected president, Joseph Seligman was offered the post of secretary of the treasury. He turned it down.

In an effort to Americanize his family, Seligman hired Horatio Alger to tutor his children. Alger proved to be a failure as a tutor. Despite the bravado of his stories,

Alger was a timid man. The kids pushed him around. He was unable to control the spirited Seligman offspring.

Every summer during the 1870s, Seligman and his family spent several months at the Grand Union Hotel in Saratoga, New York. At this time, Saratoga was a fashionable resort where all of New York City's elite spent June, July, and August. While commoners sweated out summers in the city, it was de rigueur for railroad tycoons and other nouveau riche as well as the more established upper class to travel upstate and parade in their finery while throwing away money at Saratoga's casinos.

Until his death in 1876, the Grand Union Hotel had been owned by A. T. Stewart, North America's richest merchant. Control of Stewart's vast holdings were passed to Judge Henry Hilton, a politician from New York who was a rather insignificant member of Tammany Hall, the political machine that ran the city. Hilton, an anti-Semite, ordered the managers of Stewart's hotels not to do business with Jews. So when Seligman tried to register at the Grand Union up in Saratoga, he was told that "No Israelites [are] permitted in the future to stop at this hotel."

Seligman was furious. And his fury started a national storm. The newspapers played the story for all it was worth, pitting Seligman, a powerful banker and adviser to President Grant, against Hilton, the small-potatoes politician.

The controversy pulled in others. The Reverend Henry Ward Beecher, a fiery, nationally known Brooklyn preacher whose sister Harriet had written *Uncle Tom's Cabin,* waded in on Seligman's side. Beecher compared Hilton to a "mosquito." Against Beecher, bigots like Austin Corbin, the narrow-minded president of the Long Island Railroad, supported Hilton. Corbin had unsuccessfully fought to keep Jews off his poorly run railroad line. He had lost that fight but urged Hilton to stick to his guns.

Hilton's anti-Semitic policies helped deplete the Stewart fortune. Jews and sympathetic gentiles stopped patronizing Stewart stores and the businesses went downhill.

In 1880, Seligman died of a stroke. He never did enter the Grand Union Hotel again, but his family business was later instrumental in putting together General Motors, one of the most successful car companies in the world.

Future American anti-Semitic incidents were not nearly as benign as the inability of a rich man like Seligman to register in a tony hotel. But the snobbery of small-minded men like Judge Hilton were ominous precursors to the murderous events that were to follow—events that would inspire the creation of the B'nai B'rith Anti-Defamation League.

The key incident that moved B'nai B'rith to action was the murder of Mary Phagan in Georgia in 1913 and the subsequent arrest of Leo Frank.

Leo Frank was born in Texas in 1884 and raised in Brooklyn. Before moving south, he graduated from Cornell University in Ithaca, New York. At twenty-four,

The lynching of Leo Frank in Georgia alerted American Jews to the lurking danger of American anti-Semitism.

he married a woman from Atlanta, Georgia, and then moved there to manage a pencil factory.

On April 7, 1913, Frank was working by himself in the factory office. It was a Saturday and Confederate Memorial Day, and all the other employees were attending a parade honoring the old South. While he was working, one of his employees, fourteen-year-old Mary Phagan, stopped by to pick up the wages she was owed. Frank gave her a dollar-twenty, but before she left the building, Phagan was raped and murdered and her body left in the factory basement.

Despite the fact that all the evidence in the case tended to exonerate Frank, the populace of the city, roused to righteous indignation by the local press, called for revenge to be exacted on Frank. One newspaper editorial spoke of Phagan's "hideous death by this filthy perverted Jew from New York." Another, by a Georgia publisher named Tom Watson, warned "that the Negro's lust for the white woman is not much fiercer than the lust of the licentious Jew for the gentile." Georgians later voted Watson to the U.S. Senate.

The key witness against Frank was an African-American, Jim Conley, the company watchman. Strangely enough in this case, the police, in their anxiousness to frame Frank, used a black man's word against a white man's, even though circumstantial evidence pointed to Conley.

During Frank's monthlong trial, mob justice prevailed. Outside the courthouse (and sometimes inside), men chanted, "Hang the Jew." Lawyers going in and out of the courthouse were taunted, "If the Jew doesn't hang, we'll hang you!"

The presiding judge himself admitted that "if Christ and his angels came down here and showed this jury that Frank was innocent, it would bring him in guilty."

In his argument to the jury, the prosecutor, Hugh Dorsey, offered the twisted reasoning that Jews "rise to the heights sublime but also sink to the lowest depths of degradation." Dorsey was also moving up in the Georgia power structure. He was later elected the governor of Georgia.

But maybe that was the point—trying and convicting Frank turned into an easy political stepping-stone to higher office for some. For others, conscience proved stronger than love of political success. After the trial, to his credit, Georgia governor John M. Slaton, knowing he was committing political suicide, commuted Frank's death sentence to life imprisonment.

Slaton himself almost lost his life. Only the swift intervention of the state militia kept an angry mob from blowing up his house and lynching him. He was forced to leave Georgia.

And the governor's commutation didn't save Leo Frank from a tortuous death. In August 1915, a mob dragged Frank from a prison hospital bed (he had been stabbed by another prisoner), chained him to a car bumper, and dragged him more than forty miles to a spot near Mary Phagan's house. There they lynched what was left of their victim. The lynch mob posed for pictures around the broken, hanging body. Despite the clear photos, not one of the mob was ever arrested. Even Pathe News took pictures of the hanging corpse and inserted them into its newsreel, which was released across the country.

The madness helped revive the Ku Klux Klan, the infamous secret society that infected the South with its racial hatred. After Frank's death, it held a cross-burning atop Stone Mountain in Georgia.

The terrifying events of 1913 in Georgia convinced North American Jews that they had to take defensive action against the rising tide of hatred. As a result, the Anti-Defamation League was formed to identify and combat occurrences of prejudice and bigotry. Another of its purposes was and still is education of both gentiles and Jews of the Jewish place in society and the Jewish community's work to better society.

The formation of the Anti-Defamation League and other similar organizations were fortunately timed. For, as the 1920s began, more anti-Semitic campaigns were begun. One of the most notorious streams of anti-Semitic propaganda was financed by Henry Ford, the successful car maker. Starting in 1920, Ford began putting his money where his prejudice was, printing anti-Jewish lies.

Organized to fight anti-Semitism, the Anti-Defamation League commemorated its seventieth anniversary with this poster (left), presented here by Theodore Freedman (on the left), director of the National Intergroup Relations division, and Larry J. Sachnowitz, president of the Gulf State Advertising Agency of Houston, Texas. Shown above are two of the anti-Semitic booklets that automaker Henry Ford financed in the 1920s.

Unterman Family Collection, Chicago Jewish Archives, Spertus College

As a forum for his ideas, Ford bought the *Dearborn Independent* in 1920, a small newspaper that he made a national publication by selling subscriptions to car buyers across the United States. (It also reprinted articles in booklets that were distributed internationally. One of these was called "The International Jew—The World's Foremost Problem.")

At about the same time, another publisher was distributing a piece of propaganda called "Protocols of the Meetings of the Zionist Men of Wisdom." Published in the United States under the title "The Protocols and World Revolution," this document purported to be a "program carefully worked out in all its details for the conquest of the universe by the Jews."

The "Protocols of Zion" originally had been invented by the czarist police as a rationale for arresting Russian Jews. Despite its logical inconsistencies and other obvious nonsensical warnings of international conspiracies, the *Dearborn Independent* reprinted sections of the Protocols among its potpourri of anti-Jewish tracts.

The diatribes appearing in the *Independent* helped the Ku Klux Klan in its membership drives. And the paper reveled in the fact that there was "good reason that the Ku Klux Klan had been revived in Georgia."

So for seven years, until 1927, this hate-filled paper tried to blame the Jewish people for virtually everything perceived as being "wrong" with American society. The paper ran articles entitled, "Jewish Jazz Becomes Our National Music" and "Jewish Degradation of American Baseball," topics that are obviously ludicrous to the modern reader.

In the spring of 1927, Ford was forced to desist. He was cowed by Jewish boycotts of his automobiles and the threat of lawsuits by some of those his publications had named as conspirators plotting to take over "the universe." In one diatribe, the *Independent* had named Aaron Sapiro, Bernard Baruch, Paul Warburg, Otto Kahn, Albert Lasker, Julius Rosenwald, and Eugene Meyer (all prominent Jewish citizens of the time) as planners in a plot to starve the world until everyone agreed to be ruled by Jewish bankers.

Sapiro, Baruch, and Warburg, with the help of Louis Marshall, who was active with the American Jewish Committee (formed in 1906 to combat anti-Semitism), fought back and forced Ford to disassociate himself from the anti-Semitic propaganda campaign. Ford, in the end, apologized and claimed he had not known about the material printed by the *Independent* and distributed to his car dealers and reprinted internationally.

In his written "apology," Ford claimed, "Although…the publications are my property, it goes without saying that in the multitude of my activities it has been impossible for me to devote personal attention to their management or to keep informed as to their contents…." It was an excuse Americans would hear many times from government and business leaders attempting to shirk responsibility for the actions of their underlings.

This Chicago association—the Paole Zion Group—was one of many organizations formed in the early 1900s to promote Zionism.

Courtesy of Hadassah

The women who belonged to Hadassah were influential boosters of the Zionist movement, which led to the creation of Israel. These Hadassah members (above) lead a 1919 Zionist parade through downtown Pittsburgh. Louis Brandeis (opposite), a prominent lawyer educated at Harvard, gave American Zionism a big boost when he agreed to lead the Provisional Committee for General Zionist Affairs in 1914. Brandeis later served on the Supreme Court.

American Zionism

Another important task of North American Jewish organizations has been to aid in the formation and survival of Israel.

In their long history, the Jews have been exiled twice from the area of the Middle East around Jerusalem—long ago, the ancient Babylonians conquered this area and sent them fleeing, and about two thousand years ago, the Romans banished them again from this part of the world. Since the time of the Romans, Jews had spoken of returning to this area. But it was only once the twentieth century had begun and such countries as Russia and Germany and other European nations became much more ruthless in their attitudes toward the Jewish community that Jewish settlement in Palestine became a more serious issue.

The Jewish desire to create a Jewish state in Palestine was termed Zionism. The movement in the United States started to grow strong in the late 1800s as Russia's anti-Jewish policies tightened. At this time, a group called Chovevei Zion —the Lovers of Zion—branched out from New York to Baltimore, Maryland. At about the same time, Jews in the West and Midwest joined together to form the Federated Zionists Societies of the Middle West. Their power base was in Milwaukee, Wisconsin.

The American Zionist movement received a psychological boost in 1914 when Louis Brandeis, a prominent Jewish lawyer, assumed leadership of the Provisional Committee for General Zionist Affairs, an organization that was negotiating with Turkey (which controlled the area) to allow Jews to settle there. Brandeis, who had been born in Louisville, Kentucky, in 1856 and attended Harvard Law School, was a member of the elite "uptown" Jewish crowd. His unexpected interest in Zionism gave the movement legitimacy. Why the interest in a Jewish homeland? He replied, "Gradually, it became clear to me that to be good Americans, we must be better Jews, and to be better Jews, we must become Zionists."

Brandeis was head of the Provisional Committee for only two years, but other Jews who worked with him felt that his two-year leadership had been decisive in driving the American Zionist movement forward. In 1916, he was appointed by President Woodrow Wilson to the U.S. Supreme Court.

The Jewish community generally viewed the creation of a Jewish homeland as both a way to give Jews a country that would stand up for them when they were threatened and as a means to gain more clout in world affairs. It also could provide a place for refugee Jews to go when no one else would take them in.

At this time, however, not all Jews supported Zionism. In particular, some Orthodox Jewish groups believed that a new Jewish homeland in Palestine could come about only after the appearance of a Messiah—a messenger from God who would save the world. According to this belief, if normal men tried to settle the Jews in Palestine, it would be an affront to biblical prophecies.

Courtesy of Hadassah

Courtesy of Hadassah

Some Reform Jews argued that the formation of a Jewish state was a bad idea because it would split Jewish loyalties between the United States and the new country. They believed this would give anti-Semites more support for their assertion that Jews were not loyal citizens of the countries in which they lived.

In any case, history doesn't listen to reasoned debates. Events beyond anyone's immediate control would inexorably result in the creation of a Jewish state. Hadassah, one of the most influential Zionist groups in the United States, was started by Henrietta Szold in 1912. Szold, a scholar and keen observer of the changing Jewish population of the U.S. during most of this century as well as a worker for the poor and dispossessed, was the daughter of a Baltimore rabbi. Her father had marched behind Abraham Lincoln's casket after the president's assassination.

Through Szold's efforts, Hadassah built hospitals and other institutions for the needy in Palestine. Later, during World War II, Szold and Hadassah worked through an effort called Youth Aliyah to save thousands of children from the Nazi Holocaust.

AMERICAN DAUGHTERS OF ZION
NURSES SETTLEMENT
HADASSAH

Courtesy of Hadassah

In 1912, Henrietta Szold (opposite, bottom) founded Hadassah. Her work took her on many trips to Palestine (opposite, top), and her organization also founded such institutions as the American Daughters of Zion Nurses Settlement (left).

From study to prayer to such traditions as baking challah, Jewish life in North America is alive and well.

For most American Jews, World War II destroyed any doubt that there was need for a Jewish homeland in what is now called Israel. Today, for many members of Jewish communities, Israel, its problems, and its tenuous place in a volatile corner of the world provide a central focus for their identities as Jews.

Certainly, without the spiritual and financial support of American Jews, Israel probably could not continue to exist. Organizations such as the United Jewish Appeal continue to raise vast sums of money to support this country, which has been in almost continual conflict with its Arab neighbors.

The Future of North American Jews

It is estimated that today there are somewhere between five and six million Jews living in the United States. Another 300,000 to 400,000 live in Canada. What the future of these communities will be remains uncertain. For example, between the years 1954 and 1980, while the population of the United States as a whole was growing by almost 40 percent, the Jewish population increased only 17 percent. More recently, some experts believe that the Jewish population has actually been decreasing because of a low birth rate and intermarriage with non-Jews. At the same time, the median age of Jews has been increasing.

According to Abraham Karp, a former president of the American Jewish Historical Society who has studied the Jewish community of Rochester, New York, this town's Jewish population has experienced changes similar to what other communities have already undergone or can expect to encounter. In his view, the Jewish population consists of "an American-born, suburban, numerically declining community of aging...professionals and administrators, whose religious affiliation has remained steady but whose lives are less and less directed by religious disciplines."

In other words, while most American Jews have succeeded in becoming successful members of their communities, on the whole many of these people seem to be losing their unique identification as Jews. Affluence and assimilation are eroding many individuals' ethnic identity.

What the future will bring to North American Jewry, and what new forms their faith and communities scattered across the continent will take, cannot be predicted. The Lubavitch movement, emphasizing traditional Jewish ways, has gathered strength during the past few years, and substantial Hasidic communities in Brooklyn as well as in some rural areas have increased their numbers as of late.

In addition, many Israelis as well as Russian Jews have recently emigrated to North America. How these new entrants will affect the flow of events in Jewish communities is still not clear.

But if the future is anything like the past, surprising things lie ahead.

For Additional Reading

Abella, Irving. *A Coat of Many Colours.* Toronto:
Lester & Orpen Dennys Ltd., 1990.

Blau, Joseph L. *Judaism in America.* Chicago:
University of Chicago Press, 1976.

Dimont, Max. *The Jews of America.* New York:
Simon and Schuster, 1978.

Feldstein, Stanley. *The Land That I Show You.* Garden
City, New York: Anchor Press/Doubleday, 1978.

Karp, Abraham J. *Haven and Home.* New York:
Schocken Books, 1985.

Kurtz, Seymour. *Jewish America.* New York:
McGraw Hill, 1985.

© Bill Aron

I N D E X